A History of

INNOVATION

U.S. Army Adaptation in War and Peace

Jon T. Hoffman
General Editor

CENTER OF MILITARY HISTORY
UNITED STATES ARMY
WASHINGTON, D.C., 2009

Library of Congress Cataloging-in-Publication Data

A history of innovation : U.S. Army adaptation in war and peace / Jon T. Hoffman, general editor.
    p. cm.
Includes bibliographical references and index.
1. United States. Army—Equipment—History—20th century. 2. United States. Army—Drill and tactics—History—20th century. 3. Military weapons—United States—History—20th century. I. Hoffman, Jon T., 1955- II. Center of Military History.

UA25.h675 2009
355.80973—dc22   2009024607

First Printing—CMH Pub 40–6–1

ISBN 978-0-16-084187-3

Contents

Illustrations

Foreword

Armies rely so much on past experiences to validate current practices that they are often regarded as inherently conservative organizations, resistant to meaningful change and innovation. Armed with doctrines and traditions developed over decades and even centuries to guide and sustain soldiers in combat, they have been understandably hesitant to adopt new, unproven methods of war without conducting extraordinarily time-consuming and detailed tests and reviews. Yet armies have often stood at the cutting edge of technological, organizational, and methodological change, for in the violent competition that marks their trade, survival has often gone to the smartest and most innovative force rather than to the largest or best armed one. Thus, however risky, innovation has over the ages become the hallmark of successful military establishments.

In the United States, the U.S. Army has a long history of innovation, from the exploits of the Lewis and Clark Expedition at the beginning of the nineteenth century to the medical and engineering advances associated with the construction of the Panama Canal begun at its end. But this particular collection of essays in *A History of Innovation: U.S. Army Adaptation in War and Peace* speaks to the purely military initiatives in weapons, tactics, organization, training, and other areas that directly impacted battlefield performance in the twentieth century. While many were successful, some were premature and others even failures, quickly abandoned or significantly modified after undergoing the test of combat. How Army leaders approached these innovations—how they sought to manage change—are stories well worth the telling since even those enterprises that proved problematic imparted their own lessons learned. This work then begins the important task of identifying those factors that encourage a culture of change and innovation—and those that militate against it. How much is due to institutional flexibility and how much to personal leadership are only some of the factors examined. By describing and analyzing the Army's experiences in past innovations, these historical essays can assist today's military leaders to become better thinkers and better innovators, making the past a servant of the future.

Washington, D.C.   JEFFREY J. CLARKE
1 October 2009   Chief of Military History

Contributors

Terry L. Beckenbaugh is an assistant professor in the Department of Military History at the U.S. Army Command and General Staff College, Fort Leavenworth, Kansas. He received his Ph.D. from the University of Arkansas in 2001, specializing in the American Civil War and Reconstruction. He is currently working on a book about Maj. Gen. Samuel Ryan Curtis and the 1862 White River Campaign in Arkansas.

Thomas A. Bruscino Jr. is an assistant professor in the School of Advanced Military Studies, U.S. Army Command and General Staff College. He earned an M.A. in American history and a Ph.D. in U.S. military history from Ohio University (Athens, Ohio). His publications include *Out of Bounds: Transnational Sanctuary in Irregular Warfare* (2006).

Anne W. Chapman, a historian now retired from the U.S. Army Training and Doctrine Command, Fort Monroe, Virginia, is an active researcher in the fields of women in the military and the School of the Americas. She received her M.A. and Ph.D. degrees from the College of William and Mary. She has written several books, including *The Origins and Development of the National Training Center, 1976–1984* (1997); *The Army's Training Revolution 1973–1990: An Overview* (1991); and *The National Training Center Matures, 1985–1993* (1997).

William M. Donnelly received his Ph.D. in history from Ohio State University. An Army veteran of the Persian Gulf war, he is a senior historian in the Historical Support Branch, Histories Division, U.S. Army Center of Military History, Fort McNair, District of Columbia. He is the author of *Under Army Orders: The Army National Guard During the Korean War* (2001); *We Can Do It: The 503d Field Artillery Battalion in the Korean War* (2000); and *Transforming an Army at War: Designing the Modular Force, 1991–2005* (2007).

Christopher R. Gabel is an instructor and curriculum coordinator for the Department of Military History, U.S. Army Command

and General Staff College. He holds a Ph.D. in history from Ohio State University. His publications include *The U.S. Army GHQ Maneuvers of 1941* (1991) and *Seek, Strike, and Destroy: U.S. Army Tank Destroyer Doctrine in World War II* (1985). Other areas of interest and scholarship are Civil War logistics and the Vicksburg campaign.

James L. Gilbert, a command historian now retired from the U.S. Army Intelligence and Security Command, Fort Belvoir, Virginia, earned B.A. and M.A. degrees from the University of Oklahoma. His books include *The Most Secret War* (2003), *In the Shadow of the Sphinx* (2005), and *U.S. Army Signals Intelligence in World War II* (2004).

Jon T. Hoffman is chief of the Contemporary Studies Branch, Histories Division, U.S. Army Center of Military History. A retired Marine Corps Reserve officer, he has an M.A. in military history from Ohio State University and a J.D. from Duke University. He is the author of *USMC: A Complete History* (2002); *Chesty: The Story of Lieutenant General Lewis B. Puller, USMC* (2001); and *Once a Legend: 'Red Mike' Edson of the Marine Raiders* (1994).

John R. Maass received his Ph.D. in early U.S. history from Ohio State University. A former officer in the Army Reserve, he is a historian in the Contemporary Studies Branch, Histories Division, U.S. Army Center of Military History.

Edgar F. Raines Jr. received his Ph.D. from the University of Wisconsin. He is a senior historian in the General Histories Branch, Histories Division, U.S. Army Center of Military History. His published works include *Eyes of the Artillery: The Origins of Modern U.S. Army Aviation in World War II* (2000), and he is presently completing a manuscript on operational logistics in the Grenada campaign.

Mark J. Reardon, a retired armor officer, received his B.A. in history from Loyola College (Baltimore, Maryland) and an M.S. in international relations from Troy State University. He is a senior historian in the Contemporary Studies Branch, Histories Division, U.S. Army Center of Military History, specializing in World War II and the Global War on Terrorism. He is the author of *Victory at Mortain* (2002) and coauthor of *American Iliad: The 18th Infantry Regiment in World War II* (2004) and *From Transformation to Combat: The First Stryker Brigade at War* (2007).

Wendy Rejan is the command historian for the U.S. Army Communications-Electronics Life Cycle Management Command, Fort Monmouth, New Jersey. She holds an M.A. in history from Monmouth University. Her areas of historical specialization are communications and electronics, the history of Fort Monmouth, Signal Corps research and development, and European history.

Mark D. Sherry received his M.A. and Ph.D. in history from Georgetown University. He is a historian in the Contemporary Studies Branch, Histories Division, U.S. Army Center of Military History, specializing in institutional history. He is the author of *China Defensive* (1996) and *The Army Command Post and Defense Reshaping, 1987–1997* (2008).

Acknowledgments

In addition to the authors of the chapters in *A History of Innovation*, many other experts and professionals contributed in significant ways. Noted military historians Allan R. Millett and Harold R. Winton shared their insights on innovation while reviewing an early draft of the manuscript. Eric Voelz of the National Personnel Records Center was invaluable in tracking down facts about soldiers and Army civilians. Molly A. Bompane of the U.S. Army Military History Institute assisted with photo research. Dennis Buley, Robert Giordano, Thomas N. Hauser (U.S. Army Intelligence and Security Command), Thomas Hurt, and David Noyes contributed photos and information for the chapter on airborne radio direction finding. John Moltz provided assistance on the speed shifter chapter. James T. Stensvaag of the U.S. Army Training and Doctrine Command helped finalize the National Training Center chapter. David Stieghan of Fort Benning supplied photos for that chapter.

At the U.S. Army Center of Military History Chief Historian Richard W. Stewart thoroughly reviewed the manuscript and provided valuable guidance. Others at the Center also read drafts and offered useful suggestions: Chief of Military History Jeffrey J. Clarke, Assistant Chief of Military History John F. Shortal, and Histories Division Chief Joel D. Meyerson. Under the direction of Publishing Division Chief Keith R. Tidman, staff members—Diane S. Arms, Beth F. MacKenzie, Carl E. Snyder—shepherded the manuscript into printed form.

Washington, D.C.   JON T. HOFFMAN
1 October 2009   General Editor

A History of

INNOVATION

INTRODUCTION

Jon T. Hoffman

Innovation may be defined in many ways, but simply put it is the creation of something new—whether it be a novel product or device, a different way to organize people or entities, an original process or method of doing things, or even a fresh use for an existing item. While ideas are a critical part of the concept, the term encompasses much more and requires that thought be transformed into action and practical use. Leonardo da Vinci may have conceived of a flying machine in the fifteenth century, but innovation occurred only hundreds of years later when others built aircraft that actually flew. Innovation has been a central component of mankind's history, for without it we would still be living in caves and spending everyday trying to find enough to eat. It has been equally important in warfare and oftentimes tipped the balance between victory or defeat. With that in mind, the U.S. Army Game Plan for Fiscal Year 2005 made "inculcation of a culture of innovation" a primary leadership objective.

Given its impact on profits, innovation has been a major topic of study in the business world for decades. The subject has grown in intellectual importance in defense circles with the more recent advent of the concept of a revolution in military affairs. By its very definition, revolution presupposes major changes, and most of the literature in this field focuses on dramatic shifts in the methods of waging war, such as the adoption of gunpowder weapons or Germany's unleashing of blitzkrieg at the outset of World War II. The current emphasis on Transformation encourages a similar search for extraordinary changes in capability. The advent of airmobility, described herein, rises to this level. But innovation covers a much wider range of activity, including relatively small changes that can still have a positive impact on battlefield effectiveness and save the lives of soldiers. Equally important, a number of unconnected enhancements, many of them seemingly minor in isolation, can eventually add up to a major improvement in overall capability, as occurred with the U.S. Army in World War II. Most of the innovations covered in this volume fit in this category of small but nevertheless important advances.

To be included in this volume, an innovation generally had to meet four key criteria. First, it constituted a significant change in the Army's way of doing things. Second, it proved to be effective in accomplishing the mission. Third, it was either unique or, if created at roughly the same time by other services or nations, came into being in the U.S. Army with little or no knowledge of, or copying from, the efforts of those competitors. Fourth, the Army or some element within it, not outside institutions or industry, drove development and implementation.

The few exceptions to these criteria merit attention because they round out a fuller picture of the innovation process. Neither the tank destroyer force in World War II nor the special patrol groups in Korea performed up to expectations, but these failures highlight the difficulty of making innovations achieve their desired ends. General George C. Marshall's reforms at the Infantry School, the Korean patrol groups, and the National Training Center were also not entirely new ideas, but they illustrate changes that mainly involved methods rather than equipment. All too often discussions on innovation become overly focused on the advent of new technology and overlook the vital role of other less-tangible concepts that have just as much impact on ultimate success in battle.

It might seem overly restrictive to limit the scope of this work to innovations developed within the Army, especially since the scientific community and defense industry have increasingly been the source of new capabilities. While those outside entities will continue to play an important role, the growing significance of al-Qaeda and other nonstate actors is altering the landscape of conflict. Compared to past decades when the prospect of waging a massive war with the Soviet Union required sophisticated systems and the most advanced technology available, today's terrorists blend into the population; fight primarily with simple weapons, such as improvised explosive devices (IEDs); and thus pose a different set of problems. Not only are their tactics more primitive, but the very austerity of their force (no fleets of tanks or helicopters) allows them to change their methods much more rapidly and easily. In this realm, technology is still useful but often secondary to critical factors, such as doctrine and organization. Frontline improvisation also assumes much greater importance, as we already have seen in the form of soldiers finding their own ways to defeat or defend against IEDs rather than waiting for solutions from the research and development community. The Information Age, perversely enough, is perhaps reinforcing this trend away from the primacy of technology. It may rely on satellites and computers, but the way in which these devices are used is often more critical than their relative technical capability. The side that best manages the acquisition and processing of information for its internal use, while externally fashioning public perceptions first or making the deepest impression, will often have the upper hand.

Even if one sets aside the nature of warfare today, the fact remains that it is the soldiers in the field—those who have to fight—who should play a major role in determining what equipment they need to have and how they will operate. They will not often build their own devices, as Sgt. Curtis G. Culin III did at Normandy or the men of Battery B, 8th Battalion, 6th Artillery, 1st Infantry Division, did in Vietnam. And they may not come up with new tactics or new organizational methods. But they fully understand the situations they face and therefore should drive the efforts of scientists and engineers and doctrine writers to develop the capability required to achieve victory. As the selected examples in this volume demonstrate, the Army has a long history of successfully developing new equipment, new organizations, and new methods, and has done so with a wide variety of processes. Transformation may be the latest buzzword for change, but it represents a challenge that earlier generations of soldiers and Army civilians have answered time and again. A culture of innovation is a part of the Army's heritage, and that experience should inspire those who now serve to find equally creative answers to the problems of today and tomorrow.

A soldier aims his M1 rifle during fighting in Italy, June 1944. The Garand semiautomatic was widely considered to be one of the most effective American weapons of World War II. *(George Silk/Time & Life Pictures/Getty Images)*

1

M1 GARAND RIFLE

Thomas A. Bruscino Jr.

The Springfield Model 1903 was a sturdy, accurate, reliable rifle that served as the standard infantry arm of the U.S. Army for over three decades. Soldiers carried it onto the battlefields of World War I, and it was a constant companion in interventions throughout Latin America. Everyone who used it loved it. There was nothing wrong with the M1903, but the Army hoped to field an improved model that provided more firepower.

Like most other rifles of the time, the Springfield was bolt-action, that is, after every shot the soldier had to pull back the bolt to eject the shell casing and push it forward to load the next round. The Army put great faith in the importance of the rifleman in battle and wanted to make him even more effective by increasing his volume of fire.[1] A semiautomatic rifle that could eject the spent cartridge and load a new round with no action other than the pull of the trigger would speed up the rate of fire. The most promising method for doing this was a gas-operated system. The driving force behind a bullet was the expanding gas generated by the explosion of the gunpowder in the shell casing. In theory, some of that gas could also be employed to drive back the bolt and eject the spent casing. Once the gas dissipated, a spring could push the bolt forward again and insert a new round into the firing chamber.

The Army had begun work on the concept around the beginning of the twentieth century, but developing a practical semiautomatic proved to be a difficult challenge. Although a variety of private inventors inside and outside the United States already had designed and built semiautomatic small arms for civilian use, a combat

---

[1] Kenneth Finlayson, *An Uncertain Trumpet: The Evolution of U.S. Army Infantry Doctrine, 1919–1941* (Westport, Conn.: Greenwood Press, 2001).

weapon presented a different set of problems. An effective infantry rifle needed to have enough power to inflict damage at long range, it had to be light enough for the average rifleman to carry it over long distances, and it needed to be durable enough to withstand high rates of fire and the rigors of field use. Commercial versions at the time were either too small or too fragile to handle the job.

Inventors from all over the world submitted their experimental rifles for testing by the Army. In addition, civilians and officers in the Army's Ordnance Department were hard at work on their own designs. Despite all these efforts, nothing workable emerged for decades. The task, seemingly simple, was proving extremely complex.[2] In fact, no other country would succeed in developing a standard service semiautomatic rifle by the outbreak of World War II. Since no flash of inspiration was providing a solution, the only other alternative was a determined process of trial and error.

One man, John C. Garand, would prove up to the challenge.

Born on New Year's Day, 1888, in the small town of Saint Rémi, Quebec, Canada, Garand moved to Connecticut with his family when he was twelve. He came from a modest background and had little formal education, but he was a tinkerer from a young age. Shortly after arriving in the United States, he dropped out of school and began working as a floor sweeper in a textile mill. He applied for his first patent before he was fifteen, and within a few years became a machinist at the mill. He also developed a serious interest in guns, working one summer at a shooting gallery, where he became an avid and first-rate target shooter. He joined the National Guard, but during World War I his design for a machine gun made him more valuable at home and earned him a job at the Bureau of Standards. Based on his efforts there, the Army's Springfield Armory in Massachusetts hired him in 1919. He immediately began work on a semiautomatic rifle.[3]

Throughout the 1920s, the Army tested a variety of designs, none entirely satisfactory, including Garand's. Part of the problem came from ammunition; no one could agree on a standard

---

[2] Constance McLaughlin Green, Harry C. Thomson, and Peter C. Roots, *The Ordnance Department: Planning Munitions for War*, United States Army in World War II (Washington D.C.: Office of the Chief of Military History, Department of the Army, 1955), pp. 175–77.

[3] John McCarten, "The Man Behind the Gun," *New Yorker*, 6 February 1943, pp. 22–28; Edwin Teale, "He Invented the World's Deadliest Rifle," *Popular Science*, December 1940, p. 68; *American National Biography*, s.v. "John C. Garand"; *Current Biography, 1945*, s.v. "John C. Garand."

John C. Garand tests an early version of his rifle in 1922. His persistence led to the first semiautomatic adopted by any country as a standard service rifle. *(National Park Service)*

caliber for Army rifles. By the end of the decade it seemed that the
.276-caliber bullet offered more promise for use in a semiautomatic
rifle, which compelled Garand to redesign his (though he wisely
continued work on his .30-caliber version). His strongest competition came from John D. Pederson's .276-caliber weapon. A battery of
Army tests indicated that both showed promise. But in 1932 Army
Chief of Staff General Douglas MacArthur insisted that any rifle
be .30-caliber, to match the ammunition used with the Browning
automatic rifle and Browning machine guns. Garand's larger-bore
rifle, already well-developed, took a lead it never relinquished.[4]
His advantage did not come from some leap in technology; his
designs were consistently more simple, stable, and reliable than
the competition. By the late summer of 1933 the Army designated
his weapon U.S. Semiautomatic Rifle, Caliber .30, M1. In January
1936 the Army adopted the M1 as its standard rifle.

That decision did not mean that innovation stopped. The basics
of the rifle stayed the same; it weighed roughly nine and a half
pounds, was made up of slightly more than seventy parts, was
approximately forty-three inches long, and held an eight-round
clip that loaded into the top of the gun. But over the next five years
Garand, the Ordnance Department, and various Infantry Boards
subjected the rifle to a series of brutal tests involving heat, cold,
mud, sand, rain, rust, and high rates of fire. Based on these trials,
Garand made significant enhancements to the design, including
new front and rear sight assemblies, a more durable firing pin,
improved clip action, and a better gas cylinder.[5] As he later told an
interviewer, "A rifle isn't much different from any other machine.
You can always make improvements."[6] Many of the flaws in the

[4] Julian S. Hatcher, *The Book of The Garand* (Washington, D.C.: Infantry Journal
Press, 1948), pp. 110–11.

[5] See ibid., p. 120 (some in the Army had assumed that Garand's role in the
production of the weapon was now complete, with one officer even suggesting
that Garand be let go to save the money from his salary); Infantry Board test
findings in Infantry Board Reports, boxes 1–65, Record Group (RG) 177, National
Archives and Records Administration–College Park (NARA–CP), College Park,
Md.; Engineering Branch, Industrial Service Small Arms Division, reports on tests
of rifles and rifle parts, 1925–1943, in M1 Rifle file, box 3, RG 156, Records of the
Office of the Chief of Ordnance, NARA–CP. See also Office of Under Secretary
of War, Security, [formerly] Classified General Correspondence, December
1940–March 1943, Petroleum–Russia, Rifles file, box 8, RG 107, Records of the
Office of the Secretary of War, NARA–CP; Bruce N. Canfield, "The Unknown M1
Garand," *American Rifleman*, 142 (January 1994): 46–49.

[6] McCarten, "Man Behind the Gun," p. 24.

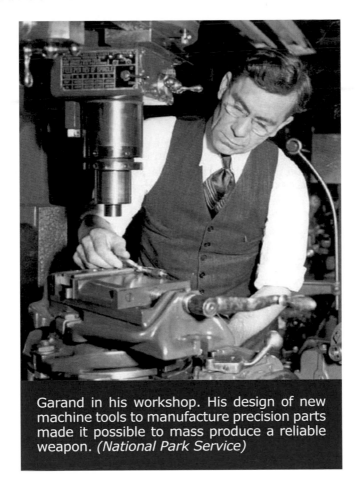

Garand in his workshop. His design of new machine tools to manufacture precision parts made it possible to mass produce a reliable weapon. *(National Park Service)*

M1 during these years came from problems with the specific and exacting machine tools necessary to manufacture the various parts of the gun. Most of the tools at the armory at the time of the initial production of the M1 were at least twenty years old, and some of them dated as far back as the Civil War. Garand tackled this problem as well, designing and building many of the tools that would be used in the mass production of his rifle.[7]

---

[7] Harry C. Thomson and Lida Mayo, *The Ordnance Department: Procurement and Supply*, United States Army in World War II (Washington, D.C.: Office of the Chief of Military History, Department of the Army, 1960), pp. 160–65. On the complexity

Even with these initial problems, the M1 began to win over many diehard M1903 proponents with its durability, ease of use, accuracy, and high rates of fire. And it outperformed all challengers, including a late charge between 1938 and 1940 from the much-heralded semiautomatic rifle designed by Marine Corps reservist Capt. Melvin M. Johnson Jr. By 1941 the Marine Corps, a stubborn adherent to the Springfield, also adopted the Garand as its standard service rifle.[8] The men of the Army's 27th Infantry Division had the usual reactions upon firing the rifle for the first time in November 1940; they found it to be accurate, with a well-designed safety, and they appreciated the smaller kick of the Garand compared to the Springfield. Lt. Gen. Ben Lear, commander of the Second Army, said, "From what everybody here tells me, this is a fine rifle. They should know."[9]

With war on the horizon, production of the Garand at the Springfield Armory ramped up slowly but steadily. In September 1937 the armory made ten rifles a day; two years later, one hundred per day; and by January 1941, six hundred a day. With the Army growing rapidly at that point, the government began placing large orders with the Winchester Repeating Arms Company. The civilian firm would produce over a half million Garands during the war, while Springfield, at its peak, turned out four thousand a day. All of the M1s produced by the end of World War II—over four million—came from Springfield and Winchester. The efficiency of mass production resulted in the cost dropping from over $200 per rifle in the beginning to just $26 per copy by 1945.[10]

---

of the machine tools necessary to produce a rifle like the Garand, see Hatcher, *Book of The Garand*, pp. 114–24.

[8] For information on the Garand-Johnson controversy and the M1 and Johnson rifles demonstration (9 May 1940 report), see Industrial Service Small Arms Division, Administrative Branch, General Administrative Correspondence, 1922–1942, RG 156, Records of the Office of the Chief of Ordnance, NARA–CP; Thomson and Mayo, *Ordnance Department*, pp. 165–68; Hatcher, *Book of The Garand*, pp. 128–39, 141–53. The softening of Marine opinion on the Garand was apparent in 1940; see J. H. Berry, "Notes on the M1 Rifle," *Marine Corps Gazette* 24 (June 1940): 24. Johnson himself wrote an article approving of the decision for the *Marine Corps Gazette* in 1941, which was reprinted in "Then and Now: The M1 Rifle," *Marine Corps Gazette* 85 (April 2001): 51–52.

[9] Anthony H. Leviero, "Men of 27th Hail the Garand Rifle After Its First Use on the Range," *New York Times*, 19 Nov 1940.

[10] For material on M1 production and on ordnance facilities expansion, see pertinent folders in boxes I-489, I-490, I-494, Industrial Service Small Arms Division, Administrative Branch, General Administrative Correspondence, 1922–1942, RG 156, NARA–CP. See also Thomson and Mayo, *Ordnance Department*, pp. 173–74;

The Garand got its test in combat when the United States entered World War II in December 1941. From the very first, officers and enlisted men alike praised the weapon. General MacArthur, commanding forces in the Philippines, reported that the M1 operated magnificently, even in constant action in mud and dirt when it could not be cleaned or lubricated for days at a time. The press widely reported his conclusions, which dispelled any lingering doubts about replacing the Springfield. An editorial in the New York Times lauded the weapon: "There is every reason why John C. Garand, if he were that kind of inventor, should put his thumbs in his armpits, puff on his cigar and say, 'I told you so ten years ago.'"[11]

The fighting on Guadalcanal in the summer and fall of 1942 confirmed these impressions. The Marine Corps made the switch to the Garand later than the Army, and production of the rifle lagged requirements early in the war, so many of the marines on the island still carried Springfields. When elements of the U.S. Army's 164th Infantry arrived to reinforce a Marine battalion in a desperate night battle in October, the marines immediately noted the difference as "the sound and the tempo of firing picked up tremendously."[12] An Army officer who fought there recalled: "From almost the first minutes of combat on Guadalcanal the Marines began wishing for a basic semiautomatic rifle. By the time we landed, we had to keep ours tied down with wire. Leathernecks were appropriating all they could lay hands on by 'moonlight requisition.'"[13] It was easy to see why. One soldier, Harry Wiens, remembered: "One excited

---

Green, Thomson, and Roots, *Ordnance Department*, pp. 58–59; Hatcher, *Book of The Garand*, pp. 119, 153; John P. McConnell, "Rifle Factory," *Leatherneck* 35 (July 1952): 54–57; and Bruce N. Canfield, "The Winchester Garand," *American Rifleman* 153 (April 2005): 46–49.

[11] For information on M1 marketing, see pertinent folders in box I-489, Industrial Service Small Arms Division, Administrative Branch, General Administrative Correspondence, 1922–1942, RG 156, NARA–CP; "Garand Rifle Praised By Gen. MacArthur," *New York Times*, 23 Feb 1942; "The Garand in Action," ibid., 26 Feb 1942; "Bataan Proves Garand Worth," *Washington Post*, 23 Feb 1942; "Garand's Test," ibid., 26 Feb 1942; "Garand Rifle Praised by Gen. MacArthur," *Los Angeles Times*, 23 Feb 1942; "MacArthur Puts O.K. on Garand Rifle in Combat," *Chicago Daily Tribune*, 23 Feb 1942; "MacArthur Praises New Garand Rifle," *Christian Science Monitor*, 24 Feb 1942.

[12] Jon T. Hoffman, *Chesty: The Story of Lieutenant General Lewis B. Puller, USMC* (New York: Random House, 2001), pp. 187–88 (quoted words).

[13] Hatcher, *Book of The Garand*, pp. 141–42. See also Gerald H. Shea, "Lessons of Guadalcanal," *Marine Corps Gazette* 27 (August 1943): 15–22.

Marine guide returned to the CP [command post] with a firm pronouncement that he was going to get himself an M1, even if he had to steal it. He had been guiding one of our sergeants, with his men following, when they met five [Japanese]. The Marine said he'd shot one, and the sergeant, armed with an M1, dispatched the other four before he could retract his bolt and chamber another round."[14]

Praise for the Garand came from all services, ranks, and theaters. Many men appreciated its power, especially compared to the smaller carbine. As Richard E. Baumhardt, a Marine officer, recalled, "Officers are only supposed to carry a carbine. But the first time I ever shot anybody with a carbine the guy kept on running. And I said to myself that is not the weapon for me. So the first man who went down with an M1, I got his weapon and kept it with me."[15] Arnold L. Crouch, a soldier, came to a similar conclusion fighting in Europe:

> My weapon was a carbine, a 30-caliber carbine—a short, light rifle. By short, I mean small. That was great during training back in the states because it weighed about half as much as an M1 rifle. But that night, out there in the foxhole, with all this activity going on you needed more power. When we went back to replenish our ammunition I found our company kitchens in the rear area and looked up one of the cooks. Their TE weapon (table of equipment) was an M1. I said, "Would you like a carbine? I'll trade you mine for your M1." And he said, "Gladly, I don't want this damn thing." And I said, "Well I want yours." And so from then on I carried an M1. I wanted something that would reach out there with a little more accuracy.[16]

The troops also appreciated the weapon's durability. A veteran said:

> It was heavy. After marching ten or fifteen miles with the M1 slung over my shoulder, the M1 became very heavy. But bless John C. Garand who invented it. The M1 took rain, mud, windblown sand, bruises and abrasions. On a few occasions I took pieces of shrapnel out of the stock, but the M1 kept on working. If you banged someone on the head with the M1, even if they wore a helmet they knew they'd been hit. The army manual calls the M1 Garand a 'robust' weapon. Indeed it was. . . . I don't know all that much about the

---

[14] Eugene H. Grayson Jr., "The 164th Infantry Regiment on Guadalcanal, 1942," *Infantry* 88 (May–August 1998): 24–29 (quotation).

[15] Robert G. Thobaben, ed., *For Comrade and Country: Oral Histories of World War II Veterans* (Jefferson, N.C.: McFarland, 2003), p. 118.

[16] Ibid., pp. 271–72.

other implements of war infantrymen might have used, but the M1 was the best thing the army ever gave me.[17]

The troops became devoted, even affectionate, toward the M1. At the end of the war Audie L. Murphy, the most decorated American soldier of that conflict, remarked: "I believe in the force of a hand grenade, the power of artillery, the accuracy of a Garand."[18] Even when the men had little faith in other weapons, especially tanks, they still gave credit to the M1. One private wrote: "It's true, all too true, that many of Germany's weapons are superior to ours, in fact, sometimes I've thought the only two things we outclass Germany with is the Garand rifle and the fighting heart of the GI."[19] It was little wonder that in January 1945 General George S. Patton declared "the M1 rifle the greatest battle implement ever devised."[20]

For his efforts, the unassuming John C. Garand became something of a celebrity. He received many awards, including the Brig. Gen. John H. Rice Gold Medal of the Army Ordnance Association for meritorious service, the Alexander L. Holley Medal from the American Society of Mechanical Engineers, and one of the first Medals of Merit from the U.S. government. His name became synonymous with what was widely considered one of the greatest American technological advantages of the war.

Garand's stature grew when he refused the opportunity to receive royalties for his invention. A New York Times editorial in November 1939 noted of the M1: "No other nation can ever use the rifle. Its self-effacing French-Canadian inventor, still an employee at the Springfield arsenal on a modest salary, has refused substantial offers both from foreign Governments and arms companies here. All his rights are vested exclusively in the country of his adoption."[21] The fact that he handed over the patent to the government earned him a great deal of credibility. Though he earned no royalties, he maintained that the invention gave him

---

[17] Jerry Countess, *Letters from the Battlefield* (West Conshohocken, Pa.: Infinity Publishing, 2005), p. 36.

[18] Audie Murphy, *To Hell and Back* (New York: MJF Books, 1949), p. 273.

[19] Hanson W. Baldwin, "Tanks and Weapons—I," *New York Times*, 5 Feb 1945.

[20] Ltr, Patton to Chief of Ordnance, 26 Jan 45, quoted in Edward Clinton Ezell, *The Great Rifle Controversy: Search for the Ultimate Infantry Weapon from World War II Through Vietnam and Beyond* (Harrisburg, Pa.: Stackpole Books, 1984), p. 1.

[21] "Our New Army Rifle," *New York Times*, 27 Nov 1939.

"a lot of pleasure."[22] When the rifle became famous during the war, he shrugged off suggestions that he should be considered a hero. When asked about the M1, his typical response was: "She is a pretty good gun, I think."[23]

The M1 remained the standard service rifle throughout the Korean War and saw duty as a sniper rifle for many years after that. Armies all over the world copied it with only slight variations. Garand himself continued working at the Springfield Armory until 1953, developing a follow-up service rifle and constantly tinkering to improve his designs. The M1 Garand, one of the great examples of Army innovation, came from hard work and constant experimentation. John C. Garand was the perfect man for the job.

---

[22] "Garand Gave Rifle to U.S.," *New York Times*, 4 Mar 1942.
[23] McCarten, "Man Behind the Gun," p. 22.

Soldiers of the 68th Coast Artillery man an SCR–268 radar set at the Anzio beachhead in Italy in February 1944. The ability to deploy mobile radar sets with troops in the field helped defeat enemy airpower during World War II. *(National Archives)*

2

RADAR

Wendy Rejan

The advent of aircraft as useful weapons during World War I led
to an immediate search for ways to provide adequate warning of
their approach, guide fighter planes to intercept them, and direct
the fire of antiaircraft artillery to shoot them down. The U.S. Army
began experimenting with various methods as early as 1918. A
number of other military forces around the world, most notably in Great Britain, Germany, France, and Japan, were pursuing
the same objective. Both the Army's Coast Artillery and the U.S.
Navy, as well as other major naval powers, were simultaneously
looking at ways to detect ships beyond visual range. All of these
efforts would go through two decades of trial and error, but by the
late 1930s a number of researchers would reach a similar conclusion that reflected radio waves provided the best solution. Army
scientists and engineers were among the leaders in this field,
though they eventually adopted the Navy's terminology for the
method and its related equipment—radio detecting and ranging,
soon shortened to *radar*. The U.S. Army's radar work would be an
important contribution to Allied victory in World War II.

    The technical challenges were daunting enough, but the
Army's effort would stumble repeatedly over the competing inter-
ests of the branches. The Corps of Engineers had responsibility for
searchlights and looked for a means to guide them rapidly onto
their target. The Ordnance Corps was interested in a way to direct
antiaircraft fire, and the Coast Artillery wanted to locate ships as
well as planes. The Signal Corps began looking at radio detection
for the same purposes because it involved electronics. At various
times each branch ran its own development program and com-
peted for extremely limited funds during the lean years of the
1920s and 1930s. Moreover, the Navy and Army independently
pursued similar efforts but generally did not share information.

    There were two basic approaches to detect distant objects. One-
way methods relied on picking up some form of energy radiated

from the target; two-way, or round-trip, techniques involved sending out some form of energy and gathering up that part reflected by the object being tracked. The initial focus was on one-way systems, since they seemed simpler and more practical. The types of radiant energy evaluated spanned the spectrum from infrared light and heat to sound and radio waves.

The U.S. Army looked at almost every conceivable approach and pursued some of them for many years. The transmission of radio messages by a ship or plane provided one possible means of location, but the target could easily avoid this by maintaining radio silence, so scientists discarded this option at an early stage. Engine ignition systems sent out another detectable signal, but that energy could be shielded at the source. Both the Air Service and the Signal Corps began looking at heat detectors in 1918 and produced a working system the following year. The Ordnance Corps picked it up but finally returned the effort to the Signal Corps in 1930. The Coast Artillery, however, kept an independent program in the same field for several more years. The interest of both branches cooled by 1936, when it became clear that the devices did not have sufficient range and were as likely to identify a cloud as a plane. Much early work also focused on sound, but because this form of energy traveled relatively slowly, it never did more than indicate where a plane had been. As the speed of aircraft increased in the 1920s and 1930s, this method grew increasingly obsolete. The growing destructive capability of bombers added urgency to the endeavor even as a solution continued to elude military forces around the globe.

The Army program took a significant step forward in 1926 when Maj. William R. Blair became the officer in charge of the Signal Corps' Research and Engineering Division. He had emigrated from Ireland with his parents at the age of ten in 1884, earned a doctorate in mathematics and physics from the University of Chicago in 1906, and spent a decade working for the U.S. Weather Bureau. Taking a commission as a major in the Army during World War I, he headed the Meteorological Section for the American Expeditionary Forces in France. After the war he joined the Signal Corps and began demonstrating a penchant for invention. One of the first devices he developed was a balloon-borne miniature weather station that radioed its information back to the ground.[1]

---

[1] *Dictionary of American Biography, Supplement 7, 1961–1965*, s.v. "Blair, William Richards"; Dulany Terrett, *The Signal Corps: The Emergency*, United States Army

Blair was instrumental in cutting off work on sound detection and focusing the Signal Corps' meager resources on heat and radio. While the former already existed in a limited but working fashion, he believed the latter held greater promise even though it remained entirely theoretical. In 1930 he became director of the Signal Corps Laboratories, a new entity created by consolidating several research efforts at Fort Monmouth, New Jersey, in bare-bones wooden buildings erected for temporary use during World War I. Blair's organization was small—less than a hundred officers, enlisted men, and civilians—and got even smaller following Depression-inspired budget cuts in 1933. The tiny outfit had to juggle many projects, and its task of locating aircraft had to compete with other priorities.[2]

Col. William R. Blair became known as the father of American radar. His development of the concept of pulse detection formed the basis of Army research in the field of aircraft detection in the latter half of the 1930s. *(U.S. Army Communications and Electronics Command)*

The Navy first verified the possible use of reflected radio waves as a detection method against aircraft in 1930, as an accidental by-product of experiments in radio direction finding. Navy scientists found that passing airplanes created noticeable interference in the signals received from the transmitter involved in the tests.[3] The process of monitoring this difference in strength in the signal

---

in World War II (Washington, D.C.: Office of the Chief of Military History, Department of the Army, 1956), pp. 31–32.

[2] Harry M. Davis, "History of the Signal Corps Development of U.S. Army Radar Equipment, Part I, Early Research and Development, 1918–1937," p. 18, U.S. Army Communications and Electronics Command Historical Office (CECOM HO), Fort Monmouth, N.J.

[3] Ibid., p. 21, CECOM HO.

came to be known as beat detection. This system could warn that an aircraft was in the area but not provide location information. Moreover, the transmitter and the receiver had to be placed far apart, because the strong signals generated by the former would otherwise drown out the weak reflection from the target.

The Army soon learned of the Navy's activities in this field, but Blair thought the utility of that method was limited. In 1934 he expanded upon the concept and described the theory of pulse detection—sending out radio waves in bursts and using the intervals to acquire them as they bounced back off the tracked object. Measuring the time a signal took to return provided a means to calculate range. Using narrowly focused antennas to send and receive the signals would determine the direction of the aircraft. He noted, however, that no radio equipment existed that could adequately perform this function.[4] The transmitters were not strong enough, the receivers were not sensitive enough, and a method to coordinate the rapid pulsing of the two devices or measure time in millionths of a second was not available.[5] The Naval Research Laboratory began pursuing the idea at the same time.

In the meantime, the Signal Corps, Corps of Engineers, and Ordnance Corps fought a bureaucratic battle over responsibility for developing this emerging concept. The War Department finally centralized all such efforts under the Signal Corps in February 1936. But budgetary regulations prevented any transfer of funds from the other branches, and the department ruled that the Signal Corps would have to divert money from its existing programs to carry on the work. In the next fiscal year Blair devoted $75,000— about half of his entire annual appropriation—to the task while still maintaining work on thirty-eight other projects that involved everything from portable radios (the eventual walkie-talkie) to sound-powered telephones, all of which would prove valuable in the coming war.[6]

By 1936 the Navy had a functioning pulse detection system similar to that envisioned by Blair, although the transmitter and receiver antennas were each hundreds of square feet in size and still deployed hundreds of yards apart, which made it impractical

---

[4] Ibid., p. 24, CECOM HO, shows Blair describing this method in his annual report submitted in July 1934, whereas Robert M. Page, *The Origin of Radar* (Garden City, N.Y.: Anchor Books, 1962), p. 36, says the Navy came up with the idea in March 1934. Both accounts avoid mentioning the other claim.

[5] Page, *Origin of Radar*, p. 17.

[6] Davis, "Signal Corps Development, Part I," pp. 32–34.

for shipboard use.[7] While the Naval Research Laboratory's program was more advanced than the Army's, for the time being the two services continued their independent efforts to achieve the same goal. The Signal Corps surveyed corporate research centers in October to see if any could take over the aircraft detection effort, but determined that its own program was far ahead of anything then under way in American industry. The Army did make use of improved radio tubes being produced by civilian firms in the United States and overseas, though it also continued to perfect its own. These powered ever-stronger transmitters. Over the winter of 1936–1937 the Signal Corps Laboratories kept developing new antennas, each one smaller and better than the last. The transmitter antennas enhanced and focused the signal they emitted, while reception antennas became ever more sensitive in picking up faint return signals.

The Signal Corps Laboratories mounted these arrays of metal rods on the chassis developed for the old sound locators, which allowed the antennas to swing and tilt easily to scan the sky. Initially, two receiving antennas were used. A tall narrow one obtained readings for the elevation or height of the aircraft, while a low wide one provided the azimuth or direction of the target. Blair's engineers also solved the toughest technical challenge of synchronizing the pulses of the transmitter and receiver. The Army Air Corps regularly provided planes for field tests of each new iteration of the equipment.

In May 1937 the Signal Corps Laboratories successfully demonstrated the concept in the field to the secretary of war, senior generals, and several congressmen.[8] The objective of the nighttime test was to guide a searchlight onto the target so that when the light flicked on the aircraft was already in the beam. The radar set achieved the goal nearly every time, though not entirely on its own as it turned out. Harold A. Zahl, one of the lead civilian

---

[7] Page, *Origin of Radar*, p. 85.

[8] Ibid., pp. 128–29, places the Navy's first successful test of a jury-rigged system on a ship in April 1937 and states that Army officials had observed these and earlier tests and that all designs were given to the Signal Corps Laboratories. Page provides no source to support his claims. The timing of the Army's successful test in May 1937 would indicate that the Army had independently produced its own working version rather than copying from the Navy in the space of a month. Even if the Navy provided information to the Army, if it merely confirmed what the Army already was doing, that would not contradict Davis's account that little or nothing came from the Naval Research Laboratory.

scientists working on the project, had noted that one searchlight in particular was most effective. After the dignitaries departed, he spoke to the corporal in charge. The soldier explained that in most cases he had been able to find the bomber in his binoculars with the aid of a local town's lights reflecting off the clouds, thus allowing him to precisely direct the searchlight. His purpose had not been to make radar look better, but merely to outdo the aviators in the cat-and-mouse game the two branches habitually played against each other. He allowed, however: "That new secret gadget is all right. Why, every time you fellows turned on the control light it was pretty close to the target—almost as good as my eyes."[9]

While the tests had not been as scientific in their methodology as planned, the radar set was proving increasingly practical. The effective range of detection had grown from a few miles with early models to more than 20 now, while azimuth and elevation readings were routinely within three degrees. It was but a short step, everyone realized, from using radar to guide a searchlight to transmitting the information directly to antiaircraft guns to aim them. Impressed by these tests, the Coast Artillery now wanted radar sets to find ships, while the Air Corps asked the Signal Corps Laboratories to develop a model to detect planes at long ranges (out to 120 miles) to provide early warning and tracking in support of fighter aircraft.[10] Oddly enough, the Air Corps had only just canceled a separate program to develop radar for use in aircraft. That concept would languish for awhile until advances in ground radar helped solve the technical challenges inherent in smaller airborne sets.

Shortly after the tests the War Department provided $200,000 for further development, the first money allocated specifically to the Signal Corps to fund radar. At the same time, the Signal Corps Laboratories divided the radio section into two groups, one overseeing traditional communications work and the other focusing solely on what was then termed *radio position finding*.[11] A mix of civilian and military engineers and scientists continued to collaborate on the effort but without Blair, who had retired at the rank of

---

[9] Harold A. Zahl, *Electrons Away or Tales of a Government Scientist* (New York: Vantage Press, 1968), p. 45.

[10] Harry M. Davis, "The Signal Corps Development of U.S. Army Radar Equipment, Part II," p. 53, and idem, "The Signal Corps Development of U.S. Army Radar Equipment, Part III, Long Range Radar—SCR–270 and SCR–271," p. 5, CECOM HO.

[11] Idem, "Signal Corps Development, Part II," p. 15, CECOM HO.

colonel in 1938. Although many had contributed valuable parts to the design, Blair's original conception and overall direction would earn him the reputation of being the father of the American radar.

While the radar team members knew they had much work to do to perfect their creation, they already had solved the vast majority of the technical and scientific issues. Now it primarily was a matter of making the equipment smaller and more reliable. Even as the demonstration took place in spring 1937 with a set utilizing three separate antennas, the Signal Corps Laboratories had a new model under fabrication that would employ a single antenna to accomplish all the tasks.

Success brought a different problem, though, since the Army chief of staff now deemed the concept so important that he thought it required much greater secrecy. During the field tests he had noted civilian vehicles parked near the base and determined that anyone could easily observe the equipment and guess its purpose. He decreed a move of the radar section to the more-inaccessible environment of Fort Hancock on Sandy Hook. The transfer and the associated construction of new facilities resulted in a delay of several months. Tougher weather conditions in the new location also hampered the work, while a hurricane in the fall of 1938 actually destroyed parts of the latest model and delayed the tests necessary to approve it for service use.[12]

The Signal Corps deployed its radar set to Fort Monroe, Virginia, at the end of November 1938 for a major series of field tests. While the device fell somewhat short of the desired goal of no more than one degree of error in azimuth and elevation, one incident highlighted a new use. A strong wind had blown a target bomber far off course over the ocean, and the pilot was lost in the nighttime clouds. The radar operators radioed directions to get the plane back to base before it ran out of fuel, thus inaugurating the use of radar as an aid to navigation.[13] In March 1939 the Army officially accepted the radar set as standard equipment, designating it as the SCR–268. The letters stood for Signal Corps Radio, a nomenclature specifically adopted for security reasons to conceal the true nature of the device.[14]

This initial model did not go into production, as the Signal Corps Laboratories continued work on a much better design. At

---

[12] Ibid., p. 45, CECOM HO.
[13] Ibid., p. 52, CECOM HO.
[14] Ibid., p. 26, CECOM HO.

The 1938 prototype of the SCR–268 radar set. This first mobile version proved effective in field tests at detecting the location of aircraft, and also led to an unanticipated new use of ground radar—to direct air traffic. *(U.S. Army Communications and Electronics Command)*

the behest of the Army, civilian firms built ever-improving radio tubes, which translated into higher frequencies, smaller antennas, and greater accuracy. The Signal Corps built the first production SCR–268 in December 1940, just three months after Germany invaded Poland and initiated World War II.[15] By the time the United States entered the conflict following the attack on Pearl Harbor, the operating forces had more than 350 sets. This device, with periodic enhancements, would be the mainstay for antiaircraft batteries of the Army and Marine Corps through 1944.

---

[15] Page, *Origin of Radar*, pp. 133–34, indicates that the Navy had tested a system meant for employment on ships in January to March 1939, had made a production decision "at once," and had 19 sets installed on ships by the time of Pearl Harbor. The Army, by contrast, had tested a set for field use in late 1938, had made a production decision in March 1939 and built the first production set in December 1940, and had 350 operating sets by Pearl Harbor. In later pages Page makes it clear that the "production" model of March 1939 underwent significant improvement in subsequent months, just as the Army set did.

From 1938 on, the Signal Corps Laboratories also worked on the Air Corps requirement for a long-range early-warning radar. This device did not have to be as accurate on azimuth and did not need to determine elevation at all, so the main task was to boost the power of the transmitters to increase distance. By June 1938 the Signal Corps had a working model that consistently located targets at 85 miles. It received production approval following field tests in late 1939, at which point it obtained ranges in excess of 130 miles. The Army designated the mobile version as the SCR–270 and its fixed counterpart as the SCR–271. The first sets were in active use guarding the Panama Canal by October 1940. Hawaii had SCR–270 units in place by August 1941.

At 0702 on 7 December 1941, two minutes after they were scheduled to shut down operations for the day, two soldiers manning one of the radars on the island of Oahu noted the largest echo they had ever seen. The range was 136 miles. Thinking the equipment was malfunctioning, they checked it out but confirmed the target. At 0720 they reported their findings to the island's air defense information center. The officer on duty, there just for training, believed it was a flight of B–17 bombers due in from the mainland and he took no action. Thirty-five minutes later, the Japanese dropped their first bombs on the vital installations and warships at Pearl Harbor. Although radar had not prevented surprise in this first battle, it had proven that it was technically ready to fulfill the task for which it had been designed. The Signal Corps would develop even better models later in the war, but the SCR–270 and –271 were good enough to remain in service till the very end.

The U.S. Army was not alone in developing effective radar equipment. The British had a system of early warning radars (using fixed towers up to 350 feet tall) in place to help them defeat the German *Luftwaffe* in the summer and fall of 1940 in the Battle of Britain. The Navy also had radar installed on nineteen warships by Pearl Harbor. Germany had functioning systems as well. Nevertheless, the work of the Signal Corps was concurrent with and independent of these efforts. Moreover, the Army's role was important, because its radar sets were mobile and meant to accompany troops into combat. This made it possible to deploy the capability on short notice wherever it was needed, including to remote and tiny islands such as Midway, where it played a part in that critical battle in June 1942. By the end of the war, Army radar systems developed for a wide array of tasks had made a significant contribution to victory.

The 29th Infantry musters in front of its barracks at Fort Benning in 1928. The regiment served as the laboratory for student officers who honed their warfighting skills leading units during force-on-force exercises. *(U.S. Army Military History Institute)*

3

THE BENNING REVOLUTION

John R. Maass

In the decade following the end of World War I in 1918, the training of infantry officers of the U. S. Army—regulars, reservists and
National Guardsmen—remained mired in outmoded techniques.
The Army's leading training institution, the Infantry School at Fort
Benning, Georgia, set the standard in its Company Officer Course
(for lieutenants and junior captains) and its Advanced Course (for
senior captains and majors).[1] In November 1927 Lt. Col. George C.
Marshall Jr. became assistant commandant of the school and head
of the Academic Department, which gave him direct responsibility
for the curriculum. He set out on a bold course to overhaul both the
method and the content of the instruction. Within a few short years
Marshall and his staff remade the Infantry School into an institution
that developed flexible, effective leaders for the modern battlefield.

George Marshall had graduated from the Virginia Military
Institute in 1901, serving as cadet commander during his senior
year and earning a commission in the infantry. He spent World
War I in senior staff positions, playing a prominent role in plan-
ning the American Army's two great offensives at St. Mihiel and
the Meuse-Argonne. His work brought him recognition from the
Army's top commanders, and after the war he was General John J.
Pershing's chief aide. Marshall then served in the Philippines and
China and taught briefly at the Army War College before taking
up his duties at Fort Benning.[2]

---

[1] A. B. Warfield, "Fort Benning, the Home of the Infantry School," *Infantry
Journal* 32 (June 1928): 573–80; Larry I. Bland, ed., *The Papers of George Catlett
Marshall*, 5 vols. to date (Baltimore: Johns Hopkins University Press, 1981–),
1:319–20; Kenneth Finlayson, *An Uncertain Trumpet: The Evolution of U.S. Army
Infantry Doctrine, 1919–1941* (Westport, Conn.: Greenwood Press, 2001), pp. 75–76;
Ed Cray, *General of the Army: George C. Marshall, Soldier and Statesman* (New York:
W. W. Norton, 1990), p. 111.

[2] *The Oxford Companion to World War II*, s.v. "Marshall, General of the Army
George C."; *Biographical Dictionary of World War II*, s.v. "Marshall, George Catlett";

Marshall had a reputation, going back to his days as a cadet, of being cool, aloof, and formal. His stiff, austere manner was forbidding, particularly to those who served under him. This distant demeanor notwithstanding, his level-headed, imperturbable attitude "compelled respect" and spread a "sense of authority and calm."[3] Although instructors and students at the Infantry School thought of him as a taskmaster, many came to praise his quiet creativity, innovative spirit, and sense of mission as he restructured the officer courses. Marshall always set high expectations, demanded results, and rewarded those who performed well. But he seemed to bring an added drive and reserved personality to his new billet. Shortly before he came to Benning, his wife had died of heart disease. Omar N. Bradley, an instructor at the school and a future five-star general, surmised that "to help overcome his grief, [he] threw himself into the job completely."[4]

In early 1927 the chief of infantry reported that he had just revised the curriculum of the Infantry School "with great care."[5] A survey of regimental commanders a few months later found almost all of them satisfied with Benning graduates. Only three lamented the overemphasis on weapons firing, close order drill, physical training, and other basic subjects at the expense of "tactics and troop leading."[6] Marshall also saw the same shortcomings; he believed that the tactical training had become "increasingly theoretical," with much of it devoted to classroom lectures on doctrinal principles and the details of staff processes, such as the proper

American National Biography, vol. 14, s.v. "Marshall, George Catlett, Jr."; Richard W. Stewart, ed., *American Military History*, 2 vols. (Washington, D.C.: U.S. Army Center of Military History, 2005), 2:43.

[3] Omar N. Bradley, *A General's Life* (New York: Simon and Schuster, 1983), pp. 63–65 (quoted words); Forrest C. Pogue, *George C. Marshall: Education of a General, 1880–1939* (New York: Viking Press, 1963), pp. 54, 286; Barbara W. Tuchman, *Stilwell and the American Experience in China, 1911–1945* (New York: Macmillan, 1970), pp. 102, 370; Cray, *General of the Army*, pp. 5, 27; J. Lawton Collins, *Lightning Joe: An Autobiography* (Baton Rouge: Louisiana State University Press, 1979), p. 50.

[4] Bradley, *General's Life*, pp. 64 (quoted words), 65; Pogue, *Marshall*, p. 286; D. K. R. Crosswell, *The Chief of Staff: The Military Career of General Walter Bedell Smith* (Westport, Conn.: Greenwood Press, 1991), pp. 79–84.

[5] Memo, Chief of Infantry for The Adjutant General, 26 Mar 1927, box 2032, Record Group (RG) 407, Records of the Adjutant General's Office, 1917–, National Archives and Records Administration–College Park (NARA–CP), College Park, Md.

[6] Memo, Col C. W. Weeks for The Adjutant General, 1 Nov 1927, box 1949, RG 407, NARA–CP.

format of a formal operations order,[7] and that junior officers, instead of focusing on how best to defeat an enemy, were sinking "in a sea of paper, maps, tables and elaborate techniques."[8] Marshall wanted them to learn the art of tactical improvisation and creativity, not rote regurgitation of standard formulas. He thought the existing infantry doctrine was too cumbersome and complicated for wartime.

Marshall intended to thoroughly revamp the program, albeit in a gradual fashion so as to minimize opposition from traditionalists. The school's commandant gave him an unobstructed hand. Marshall also benefited from Benning's favored status and his own efforts to hand-pick talented instructors, many of whom would rise to become generals.[9] The new assistant commandant launched his attack across a broad front, changing the content of the program, how the

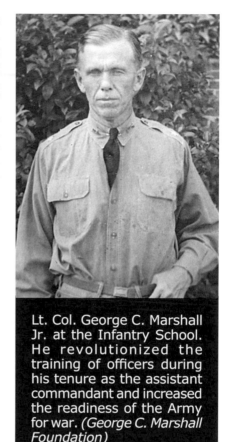

Lt. Col. George C. Marshall Jr. at the Infantry School. He revolutionized the training of officers during his tenure as the assistant commandant and increased the readiness of the Army for war. *(George C. Marshall Foundation)*

young officers applied that knowledge in field training, and even how the school imparted material to students.

Despite the chief of infantry's satisfaction with the 1927 curriculum, one of Marshall's first acts was to form a committee to rethink the entire program of instruction. Based on the group's recommendations, Marshall advocated a major shift of hours to tactics, including an increasing emphasis on mechanized warfare.

---

[7] George C. Marshall, "Introduction" to *Infantry in Battle*, 2d ed. (Richmond, Va.: Garrett and Massey for *The Infantry Journal*, 1939), pp. vii (quoted words), viii; Infantry School Annual Rpt, 30 Jun 1933, p. 31, box 2048, RG 407, NARA–CP.

[8] Ltr, Marshall to Maj Gen Stuart Heintzelman, 4 Dec 1933, in Bland, *Papers*, 1:411.

[9] Pogue, *Marshall*, p. 249; Bland, *Papers*, 1:320.

The school would also teach students how to prepare and conduct challenging field training for their own units. By the time Marshall departed Benning, the number of hours devoted to tactics instruction in the Company Officer Course had nearly doubled from 221 to 400. For the Advanced Course, it totaled almost 800 hours.[10]

Marshall further focused the tactical work on "a very practical system suited to officers who will be responsible for the development of a hastily raised wartime force."[11] The U.S. Army had faced that type of situation in World War I, but Marshall worried that the hard lessons had been forgotten in the aftermath of victory. He knew that the majority of troops in a future mobilization, even officers, would come directly from civilian life and would not have the skills and the experience to execute the type of complex operations that a professional standing army might be able to handle. "We must develop a technique and methods so simple and so brief that the citizen officer of good common sense can readily grasp the idea," he maintained.[12] He began by doing away with the production of overly detailed operations orders, arguing that commanders rarely had the time to develop and issue long written orders in wartime. He taught his officers to rely on brief written or even oral orders and stressed the use of basic, straightforward language rather than the jargon and rigid format found in training manuals.[13]

Following in the footsteps of his mentor, Pershing, Marshall was a devotee of open warfare—offensive maneuver—and wanted

---

[10] Infantry School Schedules, 24 Apr 1928, box 1948; Committee Rpt to Assistant Commandant, Infantry School, Fort Benning, Ga., 21 Apr 1928, box 519; Memo, Brig Gen Edgar T. Collins for The Adjutant General, 24 Apr 1928, box 1948; Infantry School Annual Rpt, 30 Jun 1933, box 2048; Memo, G. D. Arrowsmith for The Adjutant General, 31 Oct 1927, box 1949; Record of Communication Received from Lt Col Donald D. Hay, 19 Nov 1927, box 1949; Memo, Col C. W. Weeks for The Adjutant General, 1 Nov 1927, box 1949; Program of Instruction, Infantry School, 1929–1930, box 518. All in RG 407, NARA–CP.

[11] Ltr, Marshall to Brig Gen Frank McCoy, 13 Apr 1929, in Bland, *Papers*, 1:341.

[12] Marshall Lecture, "Development in Tactics," in Bland, *Papers*, 1:336; Crosswell, *Chief of Staff*, p. 49; Pogue, *Marshall*, p. 251 (quotation); Infantry School Annual Rpt, 30 Jun 1929, box 11, RG 177, Records of the Chief of Arms, NARA–CP; ibid., 30 Jun 1933, box 2048, RG 407, NARA–CP.

[13] Larry I. Bland, "George C. Marshall and the Education of Army Leaders," *Military Review* 68 (October 1988): 27–37; Marshall Lecture, "Development in Tactics," in Bland, *Papers*, 1:336; Ltr, Marshall to Heintzelman, 4 Dec 1933, in Bland, *Papers*, 1:410; Infantry School Annual Rpt, 30 Jun 1928, box 1948, RG 407, NARA–CP; ibid., 30 Jun 1929, box 11, RG 177, NARA–CP.

to avoid the static trench battles that had entangled the European combatants in World War I and cost them millions of casualties. Marshall was convinced that the capability to execute fluid operations would be even more critical in future conflicts. To that end, he was one of the leaders in driving the Army to revamp its organization and doctrine. He wanted a triangular structure in which each unit had three subordinate maneuver elements, a more flexible arrangement than the existing square formations with four maneuver elements. He championed the concept of the holding attack as the standard operation that commanders at any level could adapt to a wide variety of situations. While one element fixed the attention of the enemy with fire or a frontal attack, another would maneuver against a flank, and the third would remain in reserve to exploit whatever opportunity arose. He believed that any leader could grasp this simple yet highly adaptable system.[14]

To ensure that students could actually implement these concepts, Marshall moved most of the tactics course out of the classroom and into the field. Several important modifications to the program reinforced this change of venue. He placed more emphasis on using the base's infantry regiment as an element of practical instruction rather than simply a demonstration unit. Instead of watching a company or battalion execute a maneuver, the student officers now filled the command billets and led the way. To give each student more hands-on experience, Marshall argued for and won the right to reduce the size of the annual class. As a result, the young officers had more opportunities to talk through the material with instructors, whether in the field or in a classroom. While the reduction in class size at first blush seemed counterproductive since it resulted in fewer officers undergoing training, the Benning graduates, when they returned to their regiments, were expected to impart what they had learned to their contemporaries via unit schools. Thus, the overall impact of a smaller but better educated class was beneficial for the Army.[15]

The tactical problems themselves grew ever more challenging. When Marshall discovered that the instructors were repeatedly

---

[14] Marshall Lecture, "Development in Tactics," in Bland, *Papers*, 1:335; Bradley, *General's Life*, p. 66.
[15] Chief of Infantry Annual Rpt, 1928–1929, p. 40, box 11, RG 177, NARA–CP. See also Infantry School Annual Rpt, 30 Jun 1933, p. 31, box 2048; Ltr, Marshall to the Infantry School Commandant, 19 Nov 1928, box 1946; Ltr, Maj Gen P.C. Summerall to Brig Gen Edgar T. Collins, 24 Jan 1929, box 1946. All in RG 407, NARA–CP.

returning to the same training areas for field exercises, he insisted
on using all of the post's hundred thousand acres to develop the
skills of students and teachers alike. He believed that good tactics instruction "demands a wide variety of terrain and frequent
contact with unfamiliar ground."[16] For similar reasons he replaced
highly detailed maps, which were not likely to be available for
real operations overseas, with simpler ones that had imperfections
and conveyed less information; leaders thus had to look more
closely at the actual terrain and evaluate it with their own eyes. He
wanted to solve one of the biggest shortcomings in many young
officers—a failure to use terrain to best advantage in maneuvering
their unit and in positioning their heavy weapons.[17]

Marshall also put an end to what he called "rehearsed demon-
strations of tactics," adopting instead more realistic "free maneuvers," which allowed student commanders wide latitude to react
to the situations that developed.[18] He added more night training
and put the officers in charge of understrength units, thus replicat-
ing additional realities of combat.[19] In every exercise he routinely
threw unexpected scenarios or surprise situations at officers to get
them used to reacting to the unforeseen. By putting students in the
field leading a real unit across real terrain, he forced them to deal
with real problems. His pedagogical approach was not to teach
them how something could be done perfectly, but how to respond
to adversity and learn from their mistakes.

To further emphasize "the strain and confusion of the battlefield," Marshall invited senior officers to the Infantry School to
talk about their wartime experiences.[20] The program already had
a block of historical instruction, but Marshall made it both more
interesting and more demanding. Instead of requiring students
to research and write a paper on a World War I battle, he allowed
them to pick any military subject they wanted, including studies
of great combat leaders. The young officers took turns presenting

[16] Memo, Marshall for Commandant, [Infantry School], 22 Dec 1927, in Bland,
Papers, 1:323 (quotation); Infantry School Annual Rpt, 30 Jun 1928, box 1948, RG
407, NARA–CP.
[17] Committee Rpt to Assistant Commandant, Infantry School, 21 Apr 1928,
box 519, RG 407, NARA–CP.
[18] Ltr, Marshall to Heintzelman, 4 Dec 1933, in Bland, *Papers*, 1:410.
[19] Infantry School Annual Rpt, 30 Jun 1928, p. 24, box 1948; ibid., 30 Jun 1933,
box 2048. Both in RG 407, NARA–CP.
[20] Memo, Infantry School for The Adjutant General, 14 Jan 1930, box 1948,
RG 407, NARA–CP.

their findings to the entire class, which trained them not only to analyze historical examples but also to defend their conclusions in discussions with others.[21]

One of Marshall's most fundamental changes to the program was to reduce the emphasis on what was called the school solution, the pre-approved answer that students were expected to come up with when facing a given tactical situation. Instead, he encouraged the officers to generate original and even unorthodox ideas. To reinforce this, he made it a policy that "any student's solution of a problem that ran radically counter to the approved school solution, and yet showed independent creative thinking, would be published to the class."[22] Equally important, officers in the course found that they were free to "disagree at times on questions of military education, regardless of rank," in an atmosphere "of tolerance of ideas which encourages open and free discussion."[23]

Marshall set this tone by personal example. He routinely joined the class in the field and initiated impromptu debates on military topics. Often he would describe a tactical situation, then pick out one student to give an off-the-cuff oral operations order. After fellow officers critiqued it, the colonel weighed in with his thoughts. He implemented a similar program for the faculty, holding occasional meetings during the school year to review and discuss emerging tactics and weapons. His goal was to continually update the curriculum and not allow it to remain fixated on how things had been done. Marshall's tutoring had the desired effect. Infantry school students noted that the instructors were ready to look beyond existing manuals for new ideas.[24]

Marshall's reforms at the Infantry School carried far beyond, changing the approach to training officers throughout the Army for years to come: Approximately two hundred future generals passed through the course as students or instructors during his tenure. A veteran of the program remarked that Marshall had undermined the Infantry School's "complacency, renewed its enthusiasm, and

---

[21] Infantry School Annual Rpt, 30 Jun 1928, p. 26, box 1948, RG 407, NARA–CP.

[22] Bradley, *General's Life*, p. 66.

[23] Bernard Lentz, "Refreshing at the Infantry School," *Infantry Journal* 36 (January 1930): 57, 58 (quoted words), 59.

[24] Bland, *Papers*, 1:320; Infantry School Annual Rpt, 30 Jun 1929, box 11, RG 177, NARA–CP; Lentz, "Refreshing at the Infantry School," pp. 57–59.

Marshall with some of his staff at the Infantry School, including future Generals Joseph W. Stilwell *(seated second from left)* and Omar N. Bradley *(standing second from left)*. *(George C. Marshall Foundation)*

trained a new generation of ground force leaders."[25] By the time the United States entered World War II, Marshall's changes had made the Infantry School an important factor in the Army's mobilization plans. In the course of that massive conflict he directed just the type of force he had envisioned, one composed of millions of citizens. They were able to rapidly transform into soldiers largely due to the training concepts, doctrine, and force structure Marshall had advocated a decade earlier.

To be sure, Marshall was not the first military educator to improve instructional techniques or enhance the realism of military training. Nevertheless, through innovation and determina-

[25] Bland, "George C. Marshall," pp. 27–29, 30 (quoted words), 31–37; *Biographical Dictionary of World War 11*, s.v. "Marshall, George Catlett"; Ltr, Marshall to Brig Gen Courtney Hodges, 15 Jan 1941, in Bland, *Papers*, 2:389.

tion he was able to change the content and methodology of the courses available to Army infantry officers in the years leading up to World War II and thereby make his mark on an entire service. His success partially explains how the Army, which came relatively late to armored, airborne, amphibious, and other advanced forms of warfighting, was able to catch up so quickly with—and in some cases surpass—other armies around the world. The revolution that Marshall instigated at Fort Benning illustrates what a single enlightened leader can achieve when he is determined to put good ideas into practice.

An L–4 of the 29th Infantry Division flies over a battery of M2 105-mm. howitzers in England in March 1943. The integration of light aircraft into artillery units increased the effectiveness of indirect fire. *(National Archives)*

4

AIR OBSERVATION POSTS

Edgar F. Raines Jr.

Not long after American entry into World War II, the U.S. Army field artillery acquired its own aircraft, pilots, and ground crews to function as air observation posts. The primary mission was to provide flexible and responsive aerial observation for directing the fire of batteries. Although the Army's aviation component strenuously objected to this innovation, it came about due to a confluence of many factors—changes in the art of war; the evolution of field artillery doctrine in the United States; technological advances in airframes, engines, and communications; tactical adaptation to the realities of combat; the personalities and leadership skills of certain individuals; and pure chance.[1]

World War I had highlighted a key facet of modern industrialized warfare, the increasing ability of indirect firepower to influence the maneuver of ground forces. To be successful, attackers needed enough supporting firepower to neutralize or outweigh that employed by the defenders. Coordination between artillery and infantry on the offensive, however, was problematic at best because communications—in the form of pigeons, runners, wire, and spark gap radios—were so primitive. Most artillery support consisted of map fire, the only method of concentrating the fire of more than one battery. Guns dropped high explosives on certain specified coordinates for fixed lengths of time and then moved to another set of

---

[1] This account is drawn from Edgar F. Raines, Jr., *Eyes of Artillery: The Origins of Modern U.S. Army Aviation in World War II*, Army Historical Series (Washington, D.C.: U.S. Army Center of Military History, 2000). In addition, the following general works are invaluable: Boyd L. Dastrup, *King of Battle: A Branch History of the U.S. Army's Field Artillery* (Washington, D.C.: U.S. Army Center of Military History, 1993); Janice E. McKenney, *The Organizational History of Field Artillery, 1775–2003*, Army Lineage Series (Washington, D.C.: U.S. Army Center of Military History, 2007); and John B. Wilson, *Firepower and Maneuver: Evolution of Divisions and Separate Brigades*, Army Lineage Series (Washington, D.C.: U.S. Army Center of Military History, 1998).

targets, all according to a prearranged schedule that gave the infantry no flexibility once the operation got under way. Aerial observers also could control fire, but even greater communications difficulties between air and ground severely limited their utility. Although the U.S. Army achieved victory using these methods, its heavy casualties produced widespread agreement that the tactics and techniques of the war were only a starting point requiring further work.[2]

Beginning in 1929 a series of mid-level and junior officers at the Field Artillery School at Fort Sill, Oklahoma, notably Maj. Carlos Brewer, Maj. Orlando Ward, and 1st Lt. Edwin L. Sibert, developed the battalion fire direction center, which used improved radios and a standard plot to mass the fires of physically separated batteries on an unplanned target. Proponents spent much of the decade of the 1930s simplifying methods and overcoming skepticism and downright opposition in some quarters within the field artillery. By 1938 the new chief of field artillery, Maj. Gen. Robert M. Danford, had concluded that the last major gap in the new system was the lack of a dedicated, reliable aerial observer to fill in when terrain shielded targets from ground observation. Obtaining that capability, however, was an ongoing problem that proved difficult to solve.[3]

Arguments over the organizational ownership of air observers dated back to World War I. The artillery had taken the position that its own officers should serve in this role. When not in the air they would be with their regiment and thus up to date on the location of friendly and enemy forces and the ground commander's scheme of maneuver. Aviators took the stance that any individual assigned to man an aircraft in any capacity had to be trained by and belong to the aviation force. The latter view prevailed in the War Department and persisted as settled policy until 1942 despite the efforts of senior artillerymen to reverse it.[4]

---

[2] The best overview of the American experience in World War I is Edward M. Coffman, *The War To End All Wars: The American Military Experience in World War I* (New York: Oxford University Press, 1968). For the tactical employment of artillery and its liaison with infantry, see Mark E. Grotelueschen, *The AEF Way of War: The American Army and Combat in World War I* (New York: Cambridge University Press, 2006), pp.1–9, 83–141, 238–79, 343–64.

[3] David A. Shugart, "On the Way: The U.S. Field Artillery in the Interwar Period" (Ph.D. diss., Texas A&M University, 2002), provides the most detailed account of the development of the fire direction center.

[4] William J. Snow, *Signposts of Experience* (Washington, D.C.: U.S. Field Artillery Association, 1941), pp. 158–59; Rpt, Maj Gen Mason W. Patrick, n.d., sub: Final Rpt of Chief, Air Service, American Expeditionary Forces, in Maurer Maurer, ed., *The U.S. Air Service in World War I*, 4 vols. (Maxwell Air Force Base, Ala., and

The two branches also had more fundamental disagreements regarding overall warfighting doctrine. In seeking to more effectively integrate its operations with the infantry, the field artillery was pursuing a combined arms approach. Only by knitting together the efforts of all the arms, argued proponents, could the Army achieve victory, because the combat power generated by the integrated whole was greater than the sum produced by its various parts. The Air Corps, on the other hand, was seeking to distance itself from the remainder of the Army. Many air power advocates asserted that long-range bombardment, operating independently of ground forces, could deliver a knockout blow against government centers and industry, thus making it impossible for an opponent to continue the war. Centralized control of air assets under the command of an experienced aviation officer would permit their efficient employment against these strategic targets. Parceling out aircraft to support ground force commanders, as was common in World War I, would merely divert precious resources from the main aerial campaign. In this intellectual environment, aviation officers devoted their energy and enthusiasm to bombardment, and observation became a backwater.[5]

Technological development created a third discontinuity between the aviation and artillery communities. By 1938 the Air Corps was well along in the transition from biplanes to high-speed monoplanes. Since observation aircraft needed to carry an observer and a heavy camera in addition to a pilot and machine guns, they were at a competitive disadvantage against single-seat fighter aircraft. In World War I the latter type had enjoyed a speed advantage of 10–20 miles per hour over observation craft. By the late 1930s the disparity was almost 100 miles per hour. If there was one lesson that aviators drew from World War I, it was that speed saved their lives. The new chief of the Air Corps, Maj. Gen. Henry H. Arnold, frankly doubted whether modern observation

---

Washington, D.C.: Albert F. Simpson Historical Research Center and Office of Air Force History, Headquarters, United States Air Force, 1978), 1:104–06.

[5] For the aviation perspective, see Robert F. Futrell, *Command of Observation Aviation: A Study in Control of Tactical Airpower* (Maxwell Air Force Base, Ala.: U.S. Air Force Historical Division, Research Studies Institute, Air University, 1956), pp. 1–5, and Tami Davis Biddle, *Rhetoric and Reality in Air Warfare: The Evolution of British and American Ideas About Strategic Bombing, 1914–1945* (Princeton, N.J.: Princeton University Press, 2002), pp. 128–75. On combined arms, see Jonathan M. House, *Combined Arms Warfare in the 20th Century*, Modern War Studies (Lawrence: University Press of Kansas, 2001), pp. 96–104.

planes could survive over the battlefield. In 1939 he substituted light bombers in place of observation craft for long-range reconnaissance, and later he proposed using heavier bombers in this role. Arnold and many of his subordinates, however, were still thinking of the ground battle in terms of the slow tempo of 1918, for which preplanned fires based on aerial photographs would suffice. The combination of long-range reconnaissance relying on aerial photography also conveniently fit with the Air Corps' doctrinal interest in the fixed targets of a strategic bombing campaign. Artillerymen, on the other hand, believed that modern combat required an observer who could identify targets and control tactical fire while he was in the air.[6]

Artillery officers also were dissatisfied with available observation aircraft for a different but related reason. They wanted a rugged plane that could operate out of forward locations, which would facilitate cooperation with the firing battalions, provide longer loiter time over the front, and decrease the significance of an aircraft's maximum range. In addition, from an artillery point of view, a slower plane was much more conducive to scrutinizing activity on the ground. The Air Corps emphasis on acquiring the fastest and most capable aircraft worked at cross purposes. The resulting observation planes were large, heavy, complicated machines that required sophisticated maintenance and a well-developed airfield, characteristics that mandated they be based well to the rear.[7]

In 1934 the Air Corps and the field artillery began looking for an alternative aircraft that would satisfy the latter branch, but it took four years for artillery officers to discover a suitable candidate. At the Cleveland Air Races in September 1938 the Germans exhibited their Fiesler *Storch*. Much smaller than the standard American observation plane, it was slower, more maneuverable, and could operate from a much shorter field. General Danford and

---

[6] Irving B. Holley Jr., *Evolution of the Liaison-Type Airplane, 1917–1944*, Army Air Forces Historical Studies (Washington, D.C.: Headquarters, Army Air Forces, 1945), p. 60; Howard K. Butler, *Army Air Corps Airplanes and Observation, 1935–1941* (St. Louis, Mo.: Historical Office, United States Army Aviation Systems Command, 1990), pp. 160–61, 170, 174–75.

[7] Rpt, Brig Gen A. Hero, 29 Jan 1919, sub: Report of Field Artillery Board, American Expeditionary Forces, on Organization and Tactics, Morris Swett Technical Library (MSTL), Field Artillery (FA) School, Fort Sill, Okla.; H. W. Blakeley, "We Must See With Our Own Eyes," *Field Artillery* Journal 29 (May–June 1939): 215–18.

the other ground combat arms chiefs immediately pressed Arnold to develop an American counterpart. He agreed to include a token number in each observation squadron, but it took the Air Corps two years to deliver the first models of the O–49, as the American version of the *Storch* was designated, for field testing.[8]

One other possibility remained, at least until the O–49 became available in large numbers. While Air Corps design goals in the 1920s and 1930s had emphasized greater speed, range, and reliability in aircraft, some manufacturers seeking to exploit the civilian market had stressed simplicity, ease of maintenance, and low cost. By 1929 they had produced a distinctly different type of plane, the light aircraft. Planes in this class were small, usually carrying only one passenger in addition to the pilot. Consisting of steel-tube frames, fabric covering, fixed landing gear, and light low-power engines, they operated in the range of 60–120 miles per hour, which met the field artillery specification for slow speed. Only two-thirds the size of the O–49, they were more easily concealed on the ground and also presented a smaller target in the air. The most popular of the domestically produced machines, the Piper Aircraft Corporation's lightly instrumented J–3 Cub, was almost stall proof, which meant that pilots could master it with comparatively little training in contrast to high-performance Air Corps models.[9]

The Munich Crisis in the fall of 1938 suggested that a general European war might erupt at any moment. It also put great pressure on Danford to solve the aerial observation problem as soon as possible, because he saw this capability as crucial in helping the new artillery doctrine achieve its full potential. He therefore launched a two-pronged effort. He directed the Air-Ground Procedures Board at the Field Artillery School to examine the air observation problem in depth, and subsequently expanded the scope of its charter to include testing materiel. At the same time he began a concerted effort to change War Department policy. In early 1939 he approached Arnold with an informal proposal that the Air Corps supply aircraft, pilots, and ground crews for observation units attached to and operating under artillery direction;

[8] Holley, *Evolution*, pp. 60, 62–67.

[9] Devon Francis, *Mr. Piper and His Cubs* (Ames: Iowa State University Press, 1973), pp. 16–68; Hershel Smith, *Aircraft Piston Engines: From the Manly Baltzer to the Continental Tiara* (New York: McGraw Hill, 1981), pp. 191–214; Piper Aircraft Corporation, *How to Fly a Piper Cub* (Lockhaven, Pa.: Piper Aircraft Corp., 1946), p. 15.

A light plane takes on fuel at a country filling station during the Carolina maneuvers in late 1941. The simplicity of these aircraft made them perfect for the air observation post mission. *(Smithsonian Institution)*

the artillery would supply the observers. Arnold rejected the proposal. The next year Danford staffed a formal proposal to create air observation units composed of men and equipment belonging only to the field artillery. The General Staff rejected the plan on the grounds that the Air Corps had not had a fair opportunity to prove the utility of existing observation organization using modern equipment.[10]

In 1941 Danford renewed his campaign, this time with additional outside support and evidence to buttress his case. Although most Air Corps officers treated light aircraft condescendingly, some ground officers were much more conversant in this realm.

---

[10] Memo, Col F. C. Wallace, Executive Officer, Office of Chief of FA, for The Adjutant General, 15 Jul 1940, in General Headquarters, General Correspondence, 1940–1942, 665 (Fire Control Installations), Record Group (RG) 337, Records of Headquarters, Army Ground Forces, National Archives and Records Administration–College Park (NARA–CP), College Park, Md., summarizes Danford's January 1939 meeting.

Many of the latter had obtained private pilot licenses in the 1920s and 1930s. Some, such as Col. George S. Patton Jr. and Maj. Dwight D. Eisenhower, had even purchased their own planes. All of them were enthusiastic about the military potential of light aircraft. In 1936 1st Lt. Joseph M. Watson Jr. of the Texas National Guard began using his own plane to direct artillery fire during summer camp. By 1941 he had perfected his technique and made several converts to the idea of the field artillery owning its own aircraft, most notably Third Army commander Lt. Gen. Walter Krueger. Even more important, Watson had alerted light aircraft companies to a potential military market at a time when the Army Air Forces (a major command established in July 1941 that encompassed all aviation elements) was proposing that the industry's greatest contribution to the war effort would be to shut down production for the duration.[11]

In response to Watson's interest, William T. Piper, the president of Piper Aircraft Corporation and an Army veteran of the Spanish-American War and World War I, mounted a lobbying effort in the War Department. Assistant Secretary of War for Air Robert A. Lovett became an early convert of shifting production from the O–49 to light aircraft because the latter would use fewer strategic materials. When the Air-Ground Procedures Board reported that the J–3 Cub (military designation L–4) was an acceptable but inferior substitute for the O–49, Piper organized a demonstration flight of light aircraft to participate in the Army's 1941 maneuvers. Under field conditions the light aircraft, especially the L–4, actually outperformed the O–49 and gained many new supporters for field artillery aviation.[12]

Despite this evidence, Arnold still opposed light aircraft in the observation role. Convinced they would fail in combat, he expected artillerymen would then demand high performance planes to re-equip their squadrons. He believed that the simplest way to solve

---

[11] Intervs, author with Col Michael J. Strok, 30 Jun 1982, and with Lt Col Henry S. Wann, 27 Aug 1982; both in Historians files, U.S. Army Center of Military History (CMH), Washington, D.C.; Intervs, L. B. Epstein with T. I. Case, c. 1976, and with Watson, 14–15 Sep 1976, in J. M. Watson Papers, U.S. Army Aviation and Troop Command History Office, St. Louis, Mo.; Interv, R. J. Tierney with T. I. Case, Piper Aircraft Corp., 21 Feb 1962, *U.S. Army Aviation Digest* files, U.S. Army Aviation Museum Library (AML), Fort Rucker, Ala.

[12] Memos, [J. E. P. Morgan], sub: History of the First Grasshopper Squadron and sub: Grasshopper Washington Story, in John E. P. Morgan Papers, U.S. Army Military History Institute (MHI), Carlisle, Pa.

this problem was to smother the program before it started. He was so successful in the byways of the War Department that Danford, to save the initiative, went directly to the Secretary of War Henry L. Stimson. A field artillery veteran of World War I, Stimson was sympathetic and handed Danford off to the Assistant Secretary of War John J. McCloy. Another field artillery veteran of that conflict with bad memories of liaison with aviation on the Western Front, McCloy brokered a deal in early December 1941 that allowed Danford to test the concept.[13]

To lead the test group, Danford selected veteran artilleryman and light plane pilot Lt. Col. William W. Ford. In the wake of the 1940 maneuvers, Ford had published an article in the *Field Artillery Journal* that outlined the deficiencies of Air Corps observation and proposed that the artillery acquire its own light aircraft units to meet the requirement. Ford also provided the first detailed rebuttal to the argument that light aircraft could not survive in combat. The U.S. Army could not land in Europe, he reasoned, unless the Army Air Forces established at least air parity with the German *Luftwaffe*. In those circumstances, a combination of maneuverability, pop-up tactics, and close cooperation with friendly antiaircraft artillery would permit light planes to survive and complete their missions.[14]

Ford and a light aircraft advocate from the Ohio National Guard, Maj. Gordon J. Wolf, formed a planning cell to develop a training schedule, tentative organization, and test program. Maj. Rex W. Chandler, Danford's primary adviser on aviation matters and the former secretary of the Air-Ground Procedures Board, assisted them. Chandler, one of the field artillery's leading authorities on communications technology, argued vehemently and successfully that the light planes should be equipped with the latest radios. Although concerned about the weight penalty, Ford agreed. Chandler then used his close contacts with the Signal Corps to secure prototypes of push-button FM two-way voice sets just off

---

[13] Ltr, Maj Gen (Ret.) R. M. Danford to Maj Gen E. A. Salet, 28 Apr 1967, in Robert M. Danford Papers, MHI; Speech, Brig Gen R. E. Chandler, 10 Nov 58, sub: Talk Delivered at the Grad Exercise, U.S. Army Aviation Training Detachment (Fixed Wing), Gary Army Air Field, Camp Gary, San Marcos, Tex., in Rex E. Chandler Papers, MHI; Diary, John J. McCloy, 31 Oct, 1, 3, 5, 17 Nov, and 4 Dec 1941, in John J. McCloy Papers, Special Collections, Amherst College Library, Amherst, Mass.

[14] W. W. Ford, "Wings for Santa Barbara," *Field Artillery Journal* 31 (April 1941): 232–34; Ltr, Brig Gen (Ret.) W. W. Ford to author, 20 Jun 1982, Historians files, CMH; W. W. Ford, *Wagon Soldier* (North Adams, Mass.: Excelsior, 1980), pp. 105–14, 118.

Col. William W. Ford *(left)* and Lt. Col. Gordon J. Wolf, following their promotion ceremony at Fort Sill in 1942. The two officers orchestrated the successful test of the air observation post concept, proving it superior to the Army Air Forces' competing idea. *(U.S. Army Center of Military History)*

the assembly line. Thus from the very beginning of its existence, the air observation post program enjoyed the advantage of the most advanced military communications technology in the world.[15]

In line with the emphasis that Ford placed on aerial maneuverability in combat, training of the test group at Fort Sill involved showing the students, all holders of civilian pilot licenses, the extremes to which they could take both the aircraft and themselves in flight. Once instruction was complete, the group divided into two flights, one each assigned to an artillery brigade and to a divisional artillery unit.[16]

---

[15] Interv, Maj Gen W. A. Harris with Col G. J. Wolf, c. 1983, and Ltr, Ford to author, 20 Jun 1982, Historians files, CMH.

[16] Interv, R. J. Tierney with Lt Col T. F. Schirmacher, Mar 1962, *U.S. Army Aviation Digest* files, AML; Rpt, Lt Col W. W. Ford, Director, Air Training, to

The tests, conducted in March and April 1942, exercised the procedures and techniques that the pilots and ground crew would have to use in coordination with firing battalions in combat, but also incorporated head-to-head competition. The flight assigned to support divisional artillery conducted a shoot off with an Army Air Forces observation squadron. In this evaluation, field artillery aerial observer 1st Lt. Robert W. Cassidy obtained dramatically better results, both in speed and accuracy, in directing fire. A second contest pitted fighter planes equipped with gun cameras against the flight assigned to the artillery brigade. The resulting film graphically illustrated the vulnerability of light aircraft, but the camera mounted on an antiaircraft gun at the artillery landing strip demonstrated that in making attack runs the fighters had been vulnerable to ground fire. The results provided evidence to support both sides, but most senior ground officers embraced the air observation posts. General Krueger wrote a particularly strong endorsement.[17]

One last hurdle remained, namely, Army Ground Forces commander Lt. Gen. Lesley J. McNair, a field artilleryman and one of the most trusted advisers of Army Chief of Staff General George C. Marshall Jr. Although McNair had high regard for Ford (who had served directly under him in the late 1920s), he was not convinced that the Army Air Forces observation squadrons had received a fair test, and he also needed General Arnold's cordial cooperation in training ground forces to deal with hostile aviation. As chance would have it, however, McNair was away on an inspection when the test results arrived at Army Ground Forces. The command's chief of staff, Brig. Gen. Mark W. Clark, who had observed some of the tests and even taken an orientation ride with Ford in a light plane, endorsed them favorably to the War Department. Marshall approved the proposal on 6 June 1942.[18]

The program assigned a section (two planes, two pilots, and at least three ground support personnel) as an organic part of

---

Commandant, FA School, 30 Apr 1942, sub: Rpt Test of Organic Air Observation for FA: Training Phase, Fort Sill, Okla., 15 Jan–28 Feb 42, Historians files, CMH.

[17] Interv, Laurence Epstein with Col D. L. Bristol, 1 Jul 1975, U.S. Army Aviation and Troop Command History Office, St. Louis, Mo.; Intervs, author with Col R. F. Cassidy, 29 Jan 1991, and with Lt Gen R. R. Williams, 20 Feb 1991, Historians files, CMH.

[18] Memo Slip, Maj Gen M. W. Clark for Secretary, Headquarters, Army Ground Forces (HQ AGF), 30 Apr 42, sub: Service Test of Organic Air Observation for FA, in HQ AGF, General Correspondence, 1942–1948, 353/1 (Restricted) (FA Air Observation), RG 337, NARA–CP; Ford, *Wagon Soldier*, pp. 125–27.

each firing battalion, each higher artillery headquarters, and each artillery staff section at the corps level and above. Over the next several months Ford established a training base, organized sections, and created a logistical system to supply them in the field. Throughout this period he had to endure constant sniping from the Army Air Forces, which had the unintended effect of making McNair a strong supporter. Ford was also under great pressure to send crews into combat as quickly as possible.[19]

On 9 November 1942 three L–4s took off from the aircraft carrier *Ranger* to support the invasion of North Africa. Friendly fire caused the first to crash on the beach, while enemy antiaircraft fire brought down the second. The third plane reached its destination, an improvised landing field at a racetrack, but when the pilot took off on an observation mission, more friendly fire forced him to return. The Army had rushed the aircraft into the invasion force without the opportunity to train with the ground troops, who were prone to shoot first at any strange plane that might be a threat. Over the next several months intensive air-ground training solved that problem, but the next commitment of air observation posts to combat in southern Tunisia produced an even more disturbing result. During the entire campaign, artillery battalions conducted only one observed-fire mission using an L–4. Soldiers on the ground understood the reasons. The terrain—isolated hills rising from a flat plain—was ideal for ground observers, while the pop-up tactics taught at Fort Sill proved singularly unsuited in these circumstances. Only the forceful support of McCloy prevented the termination of the program at this point.[20]

Morale among pilots and ground crewmen fell because of the perception that they were being misused. Then their logistical system, which worked well enough in the United States, broke down completely. In an effort to remedy the situation, the II Corps artillery officer, Col. Charles E. Hart, attached a young air observation post pilot, 1st Lt. Delbert L. Bristol, to his staff. A hard-charging

[19] Memo, Brig Gen I. H. Edwards, Assistant Chief of Staff, G–3, War Department General Staff, for Commanding General, AGF, 6 Jun 1942, sub: Organic Air Observation for FA, Microfilm A1387, U.S. Air Force Historical Research Agency, Maxwell Air Force Base, Ala.

[20] Edgar F. Raines Jr. "Disaster Off Casablanca: Air Observation Posts in Operation Torch and the Role of Failure in Institutional Innovation," *Air Power History* 49 (Fall 2002): 18–33; Paul A. DeWitt, "The Air OP of the Armored Artillery," *Military Review* 24 (September 1944): 33–34; O. W. Martin, "Armored Artillery at Sened Station," *Field Artillery Journal* 33 (August 1943): 569–72.

Missouri National Guardsman who had served as Ford's adjutant, Bristol cobbled together enough supplies to keep the planes in the air, bucked up morale, fired two nonperforming pilots, and junked pop-up tactics in favor of extended aerial patrols of the front. His performance was so successful that Hart gave him permanent responsibility over administrative and logistical support and technical supervision of all air sections assigned to the corps. In the process Bristol created a model copied by all other artillery sections at echelons above divisions. More important, his reforms produced immediate results in combat. When II Corps shifted to the mountainous central Tunisian front and joined in the Allied offensive that culminated in the German surrender in North Africa, air observation posts proved indispensable in breaking through the enemy defenses. Thereafter, the field artillery could not get enough light aircraft, and other ground arms coveted them as well. Hart, subsequently a lieutenant general, credited Bristol more than any other individual for the success of air observation posts in combat during World War II. [21]

Air observation posts became an integral part of the U.S. Army's artillery system between 1942 and 1945. Only the British Army had anything at all comparable, but it pursued a much different organizational philosophy. The British squadrons, which had developed independently and parallel to the American effort, consisted of mixed Royal Artillery and Royal Air Force personnel and were assigned only at corps level. Their impact was limited by their smaller numbers and organizational distance from frontline units. [22]

In World War II American air observation posts were deeply imbedded in the combined arms team, enhancing the effectiveness of artillery support to infantry, armor, and other combat units. Occasionally, they played a major role—as at Anzio in 1944 where aerial observers prevented the Germans, who held all the high ground, from gaining a major advantage over Allied forces in the beachhead. For the most part, they served a less sensational but

<hr>

[21] Intervs, author with Strok, 30 Jun 1982; Rpt, Col C. E. Hart, Artillery Officer, II Corps, to CG, AGF, [1943], sub: Employment of Artillery of the II Corps during the N Tunisian Campaign Ending in the Capture of Bizerte and the Surrender of the German Forces in N Africa, in II Corps Artillery, "Employment of Field Artillery of II Corps in Northern Tunisian Campaign," Miscellaneous Bound Ms, MSTL, FA School.

[22] H. J. Parham and E. M. G. Belfield, *Unarmed Into Battle: The Story of the Air Observation Post* (Winchester, U.K.: Wykeham Press, 1956), pp. 17–29.

still valuable function. Luck, widespread recognition in professional circles of a serious tactical shortcoming, the ready availability of off-the-shelf technology, and input from a number of fathers gave birth to this tactical-technical-organizational innovation that proved to be one of several key elements that enabled American artillery to dominate its counterparts in the Axis armies.[23]

---

[23] For an account of the role of air observation posts at Anzio, see Interv, Col B. R. Kramer and Lt Col R. K. Andreson with Brig Gen O. G. Goodhand, 9 May 1978, MHI; Interv, author with Col J. W. Oswalt, 13 Jan 1982, Historians files, CMH; Ltr, Lt A. W. Schultz to Capt B. A. Devol, IX Corps Artillery Air Officer, n.d., in Memo, Lt Col G. J. Wolf, 15 Jun 44, sub: Informal Information, in Field Artillery School, Department of Air Training, "Training Memoranda," Miscellaneous Bound Ms, MSTL, FA School.

M4 medium tanks line a street in Luneville, France, in the fall of 1944. While it was no match individually for most German tank models, the mass-produced Sherman, coupled with a better armored force organization and combined arms tactics, played a substantial role in achieving victory. *(National Archives)*

5

ARMORED FORCE ORGANIZATION

Mark D. Sherry

The U.S. Army lacked a useful armored capability in its arsenal at the outset of World War II in September 1939. The National Defense Act of 1920 had deactivated the fledgling Tank Corps and assigned responsibility for developing armored forces to the infantry, although in practice the cavalry also fielded its own mechanized units. The two branches worked independently, developing competing equipment and doctrine. Bureaucratic inertia and infighting, coupled with a lack of resources, resulted in meager armored forces built around a mix of outmoded World War I–era tanks and a handful of experimental vehicles. The German blitzkrieg across the Low Countries and France in May 1940 served as a clarion call to change. Fortunately, before undertaking its first armored operations in North Africa in November 1942, the U.S. Army benefited from more than three years of observation of the main European belligerents. But instead of merely copying, the Americans improved upon what they saw, particularly in the areas of unit organization and training.[1]

Germany was the clear leader in armored warfare in the early years of World War II, organizing and training to conduct mobile operations as a cohesive combined arms force. As the U.S. Army's Armored Force commander, Maj. Gen. Adna R. Chaffee, noted to Congress in April 1941, "The success of the German armored tactics has as we know been great and has rendered obsolete the tactical procedures of World War I."[2] Although the structure of

---

[1] Marvin A. Kreidberg and Merton G. Henry, *History of Military Mobilization in the United States Army, 1775–1945* (Washington, D.C.: Department of the Army, 1955), pp. 480–90, 554–80, 587–98; Robert Stewart Cameron, "Americanizing the Tank: U.S. Army Administration and Mechanized Development within the Army, 1917–1943" (Ph.D. diss., Temple University, 1994), pp. 274–327.

[2] Statement of Maj Gen Adna R. Chaffee, Commanding General of the Armored Force, United States Army, to the Subcommittee of the Committee

German armored divisions varied, the units typically fielded a regiment of three tank battalions, a motorized infantry brigade of two regiments (two battalions each), and a regiment of primarily towed artillery. (A motorized unit traveled to the battlefield in soft vehicles, such as trucks, and dismounted to fight on foot. A mechanized, or armored unit, in contrast, could fight from its vehicles, which boasted armor protection.) The Germans often task-organized below the division level, with tank and infantry regimental headquarters swapping some subordinate units and controlling/ maintaining the resulting combined arms forces.

German innovation in doctrine and organization more than offset the raw numerical, and sometimes qualitative, superiority in tanks enjoyed by Great Britain and France. Early in the war British armored divisions had two armored brigades (three tank battalions each) and one support group (two motorized infantry battalions and one artillery battalion). The tank-heavy organization was primarily designed to breach strong defensive positions, much as armor had been used in World War I. Unlike its German counterpart, it was not intended to be an independent force for exploiting a breakthrough. British commanders also tended to fight as they were organized, employing their armor and support brigades on separate missions without any cross-attachment. The French had developed light mechanized divisions to carry out advance guard and screening missions, thus augmenting their horse cavalry, but they did not begin to organize armored divisions until the war was under way and then concentrated on a role similar to the British.[3]

The U.S. Army's interest in armored forces during the interwar years had been limited, in part by its focus on fighting a future war primarily with infantry as the main maneuver arm supported by field artillery. While the infantry espoused a doctrine of medium

---

on Appropriations, Apr 1941, pp. 3–12 (quotation), copy in Combined Arms Research Library, U.S. Army Command and General Staff College (CGSC), Fort Leavenworth, Kans. (hereinafter cited as Chaffee Statement); "The Armored Force Command and Center," Army Ground Forces (AGF) Study No. 27, 1946, pp. 5–6, AGF Historical Section, copy in U.S. Army Center of Military History, Washington, D.C.

[3] Bruce I. Gudmundsson, *On Armor* (Westport, Conn.: Praeger, 2004), pp. 60–63, 83–96, 135–37; Richard M. Ogorkiewicz, *Armor: A History of Mechanized Forces* (New York: Frederick A. Praeger, 1960), pp. 59–60, 65–68, 73–77; Ian V. Hogg, *Armor in Conflict* (London: Jane's Publishing, 1980), pp. 88–94; Chaffee Statement, pp. 3–12, CGSC.

and heavy tanks providing support in penetrating enemy strong-points, the cavalry emphasized using light tanks and armored cars to conduct its traditional reconnaissance missions, pursuit of fleeing enemies, and exploitation of breakthroughs.

In addition to differing missions, the two branches instilled a different ethos in their armored leaders. The mechanized cavalry adhered to a "raise pistol and charge" philosophy; the infantry-tank school embraced a more plodding "look before you leap" attitude. For a brief period in 1930–1931, the Army fielded a mechanized force that tested a combined arms approach to armored warfare. The organization's commander came from the cavalry and its executive officer from the infantry. Army Chief of Staff General Douglas A. MacArthur ended the experiment, however, directing that each branch mechanize its operations in accordance with the requirements of its independent mission. The War Department lacked a means not only to integrate and reconcile the infantry and cavalry schools but also to evaluate and borrow from foreign innovations. In at least one respect, this oversight proved academic. The Army's budget for armored forces averaged only about $167,000 per year between 1920 and 1932, an era in which one Mark VIII medium tank cost $85,000.[4]

Mobilization for the emergency occasioned by the war in Europe caused the U.S. Army to expand and focus its mechanized forces. The Third Army maneuvers in the spring of 1940 offered proponents of armored warfare the opportunity they had awaited for years. The 7th Cavalry Brigade (Mechanized), commanded by then-Brig. Gen. Chaffee, and the infantry's Provisional Tank Brigade, commanded by Brig. Gen. Bruce Magruder, operated together for the first time as a makeshift division. At the debriefing at the end of the of the exercises Chaffee, Magruder, and other tank advocates, including Cols. Alvan C. Gillem and George S. Patton Jr., confronted the War Department's Assistant Chief of Staff G–3 Maj. Gen. Frank M. Andrews.

Chaffee had first gotten involved with mechanized forces in May 1928 as a staff officer in the War Department's G–3 section, thereafter serving in a succession of assignments pivotal

---

[4] Cameron, "Americanizing the Tank," pp. 9–16, 26–28, 32, 56–61, 74–91, 223–46; John B. Wilson, *Maneuver and Firepower: The Evolution of Divisions and Separate Brigades* (Washington, D.C.: U.S. Army Center of Military History, 1998), pp. 121–25; "The Armored Force Command and Center," pp. 1–5, 13–14, 16 (quoted words), 17.

to armor developments. In between two mechanized command assignments at Fort Knox, Chaffee had served as head of the War Department's Budget and Legislative Liaison Branch, where he played a direct role in ensuring that the fledgling mechanized and armored forces did not come up completely empty handed in the struggles to apportion the Army's meager interwar funds. Although Patton had commanded a brigade in the American Expeditionary Forces' Tank Corps in France, he reverted to cavalry service during the interwar period. Indeed, while serving in the Office of the Chief of Cavalry in 1930, he authored an article in *Cavalry Journal* that had challenged some of the more enthusiastic claims of armor advocates that mechanized units would soon replace the horse cavalry on the battlefield. But with the war in Europe having validated armored warfare, Patton proved once again a zealous promoter of armored forces. The arguments made by Chaffee, Patton, and others at the end of the maneuvers found a ready audience in Andrews. Having served as an aviator for over two decades and as the first commander of General Headquarters Air Force, Andrews understood the rationale that consolidation of effort and forces provided the best means to exploit the potential of weapons subject to rapidly developing technology.[5]

The consensus that emerged from this meeting in a schoolhouse in Louisiana was that the Army had to unify its existing tank and mechanized cavalry forces. The cavalry and infantry branches had followed too conservative a course, and both branch chiefs remained more interested in subordinating tank and mechanized units to their own mobilization plans than exploiting the full potential of such supporting weapons. The tank enthusiasts argued that the solution to the Army's inertia was a new combined arms command with the authority to organize and train all armored units under one roof, thus breaking them free from the limitations of the traditional branches.[6]

Andrews took these recommendations back to Washington. Undaunted by the objections of both cavalry and infantry branch

---

[5] Cameron, "Americanizing the Tank," pp. 45–47, 51–55, 82–83.

[6] John B. Wilson, "Organizing the First Armored Divisions: The Meeting at a Schoolhouse in Louisiana in 1940 Dragged the Infantry and Cavalry Branches Into the Age of Combined Arms," *Armor* 108 (July–August 1999): 41–43; Timothy K. Nenninger, "Organizational Milestones in the Development of American Armor, 1920–40," in George F. Hofmann and Donn A. Starry, eds., *Camp Colt to Desert Storm: The History of U.S. Armored Forces* (Lexington: University Press of Kentucky, 1999), pp. 57–60; Cameron, "Americanizing the Tank," pp. 684–93.

chiefs, he recommended establishment of permanent mechanized divisions. Andrews hosted a conference in June to discuss the organization of these new divisions, and divulged that they would fall under control of a command independent of the existing branches. On 10 July 1940 Army Chief of Staff General George C. Marshall Jr. established the Armored Force, selecting Chaffee as commanding general. Amalgamating the existing tank and mechanized cavalry units, the new organization assumed responsibility for developing doctrine and for training both units and individuals. It was a new branch in everything but name, though it combined elements of nearly all arms.[7]

The Armored Force quickly became immersed in trying to catch up with European armies as it organized, equipped, and trained the first U.S. armored units. The glue needed to meld these outfits into a cohesive team and ensure that they succeeded on the battlefield was an effective warfighting doctrine. One of Chaffee's first decisions was that armored units should operate as a combined arms force designed for rapid offensive operations, especially against enemy flanks. Rather than support infantry units in breaching prepared positions, armored units would exploit such penetrations, moving decisively to crush units in the enemy rear areas through shock, mobility, and firepower.[8] From the Germans, the Army's early armor leaders also adopted one key leadership tenet—"the necessity for allowing small unit commanders to proceed on their own initiative after orders outlining the battle plan had been issued by higher headquarters."[9]

Although the Army initially established four armored corps, the tactical building block for armored forces was the division. The War Department approved the activation of the first two armored divisions in July 1940, issuing tables of organization for these units in November. The early divisions had 12,697 men organized in one armored brigade (two light armored regiments, one medium armored regiment, and one field artillery regiment), an infantry regiment, a separate field artillery battalion, and supporting units. The light and medium armored regiments differed in the size of

---

[7] "Armored Force Command and Center," pp. 9–11; Chaffee Statement, pp. 14–17, CGSG. The choice of the term *armor* to denote the force was apparently a compromise between the chief of infantry, who objected to the term *mechanized*, and the chief of cavalry, who similarly objected to the term *tank* in the title.

[8] Chaffee Statement, p. 19, CGSG; "Armored Force Command and Center," pp. 13–14, 16–17.

[9] "Armored Force Command and Center," pp. 18, 22–26, 27 (quotation), 28.

A unit mounted on half-tracks pauses near El Guettar, Tunisia, in March 1943. The decision to give armored infantrymen cross-country mobility and armor protection enabled them to fight alongside tanks. *(National Archives)*

tank they possessed. Unlike European divisions that normally had truck-mounted infantry and towed artillery, all infantrymen in the U.S. armored division were mounted in half-tracks, and all artillery was self-propelled. This was the first important American innovation, making it possible for all elements of the armored force to maneuver and fight together with similar mobility and at least some measure of armor protection.

From the outset, the Armored Force identified training and development of leaders as a major issue. It sought to amalgamate officers that had served in mechanized cavalry and infantry units, developing a new armored concept of fighting in the process. Spurred by lessons learned and observer reports from Allied forces in the European theater, the Armored Force adjusted its training programs in conjunction with changes in tactics, techniques, and procedures. The training of armored soldiers, intense and lengthy, increased from twenty-six to thirty-eight weeks in early 1943. The investment in combined arms training starting at the individual level fostered a team outlook that percolated throughout the force.[10]

American armored forces performed poorly in their first real battle against the enemy, at Kasserine Pass in February 1943. But the fault had nothing to do with the U.S. Army's concept. The 1st Armored Division had sailed for Europe in May 1942 shortly after receiving "a massive infusion of recently inducted replacement troops."[11] During the five months before it landed in North Africa as part of Operation Torch, the division conducted mostly badly needed individual training and very few unit exercises. Compared to the German panzer forces at Kasserine, the Americans lacked combat experience, had less effective tanks and antitank guns, suffered from weak leadership at senior levels, and received almost no air support. Battle weeded out the incompetent and hardened the survivors, better weapons already were in the pipeline, and the Army Air Forces would cooperate more closely with the ground forces. Although the M4 Sherman tank would never be a match one-on-one with German panzers, the Armored Force did not need to rethink its basic approach and the overall effectiveness of America armored divisions would become apparent in subsequent rematches with the German army.

During the war two major reorganizations of the armored division occurred. The first, in March 1942, eliminated the armored brigade headquarters and created two new headquarters, Combat Commands A and B, each headed by a brigadier general with a small staff. The artillery regiment headquarters also disappeared, with all batteries in the division reshuffled into three separate battalions. Army Ground Forces commander Lt. Gen. Lesley J. McNair directed the second major redesign in September 1943, which eliminated the other regimental headquarters, pared the division's strength to 10,937 men and 263 tanks, and organized the combat elements into nine separate battalions—three armored (each with one light and three medium tank companies), three armored infantry, and three armored field artillery. With the regimental structure

---

[10] Ibid., pp. 18–19, 53–54, 81–82; Cameron, "Americanizing the Tank," p. 885.

[11] Martin Blumenson, "Kasserine Pass, 30 January–22 February 1943," in *America's First Battles, 1776–1965*, ed. Charles E. Heller and William A. Stofft (Lawrence: University Press of Kansas, 1986), p. 235.

abolished, all supply and maintenance support resided at battalion and division level. (Two of the oldest armored divisions, however, retained a structure of two armored regiments and one armored infantry regiment for the rest of the war).[12]

Although a number of factors drove the 1943 reorganization, including span of control problems and a desire to reduce the road space occupied by a division on the move, the most significant outcome was a highly flexible tactical organization. The division commander assigned armored, armored infantry, armored field artillery, and supporting units to each combat command based on mission and other requirements.[13] The result was a combined arms team below division that was task-organized and able to expand and contract with an ever-changing set of subordinate units in response to specific situations.

Moreover, the combat command headquarters was a strictly tactical headquarters, unlike the regiment which had retained administrative and support responsibilities. Consequently, the division commander could attach or detach maneuver or artillery battalions to a combat command without significant logistical planning or tailoring of supporting units; that responsibility remained at the battalion and division level. As important, the combat command headquarters were staffed and trained to fight a combined arms battle and focus solely on tactical issues. By contrast, when a German panzer division task-organized, a tank or infantry regiment headquarters had to become a combined arms tactical echelon while still retaining its administrative and logistical responsibilities as a single-branch command.[14] The U.S. armored division structure thus proved more compatible with the requirements of combined arms warfare.

As the war progressed, some U.S. Army armored division commanders in Europe further task-organized their forces. By late 1944 a number of divisions had expanded the reserve command, Combat Command R, into a full tactical command. Other divisions also task organized armor and armored infantry battalions at the company level and below on a combined arms basis, especially during exploitation and pursuit operations, affording

---

[12] Wilson, *Maneuver and Firepower*, pp. 147–52; "Armored Force Command and Center," pp. 29–40; Wilson, "Organizing the First Armored Divisions," pp. 41–43.

[13] Wilson, *Maneuver and Firepower*, pp. 184–87.

[14] "Armored Force Command and Center," pp. 41–43; Cameron, "Americanizing the Tank," pp. 765–70, 890.

An M8 75-mm. self-propelled howitzer lends support to an attack in France. With the creation of the combat command headquarters and the elimination of the regimental echelon, U.S. Army armored divisions had the most flexible and effective armored task organization employed by any nation in World War II. *(National Archives)*

maximum flexibility at the lowest level and decentralized decision making.[15]

Time and again, operations in Europe vindicated the flexibility of the armored division's design. In the weeks immediately after the Allied invasion of Normandy, the U.S. First Army used elements of three armored divisions in limited infantry support roles. During the breakout from the Normandy beachhead in late July and August, however, armored units were able to conduct the kind of exploitation operations championed by early mechanized cavalry proponents. The combined power of tanks, armored infantry, armored artillery, and mechanized supporting units smoothed the advance, with each arm contributing its unique capability

---

[15] "Armored Force Command and Center," pp. 34–36, 48–49.

when the situation required it. The 6th Armored Division commander, Maj. Gen. Robert W. Grow, initially had to convince the
skeptical VIII Corps commander, Maj. Gen. Troy H. Middleton, of
the advantages of unleashing his division for exploitation operations if the breakthrough in Operation Cobra in late July proved
successful. The success of the 6th Armored Division's initial drive
to Avranches on the boundary between Normandy and Brittany
apparently overcame opposition in VIII Corps and Middleton's
infantry bias. When VIII Corps fell under Third Army command
at the beginning of August, Middleton responded to orders to
capture the port of Brest as soon as possible by permitting Grow
to bypass any major opposition on his way to Brest. Grow inter-
preted his orders to permit him to deviate from assigned routes
as the tactical situation dictated. He thus directed his two combat commands to proceed on separate routes to Brest, arriving on
8 August and bottling German forces inside the port until additional VIII Corps troops could arrive.[16]

Later operations demonstrated that the combat command structure was capable of even more independent self-sustaining operations. For example, the 4th Armored Division commander, Maj.
Gen. John S. Wood, persuaded his corps commander to allow him
to split his division, with each combat command supporting a different infantry division in crossing the Moselle River in September
1944. The two combat commands conducted a double envelopment
of the city of Nancy, linking up near the village of Arracourt on 16
September and cutting off elements of two German divisions.[17]

General George S. Patton assessed the value of armored forces
at the end of the war. In contrast to the infantry division, where
"the purpose of the tanks is to get the infantry forward," he pointed
out that the armored division used its infantry "to break the tanks
loose." He went on to note: "The enemy's rear is the happy hunt-
ing ground for armor." Although he believed that there were
clearly defined missions for tanks in each arm, Patton's forces had
exploited the flexibility of armored divisions on numerous occasions to accomplish both purposes.[18]

---

[16] George F. Hofmann, *The Super Sixth: History of the 6th Armored Division in
World War II and Its Post-war Association* (Louisville, Ky.: Sixth Armored Division
Association, 1975), pp. 56–96.

[17] Don M. Fox, *Patton's Vanguard: The United States Army Fourth Armored
Division* (Jefferson, N.C.: McFarland, 2003), pp. 101–23.

[18] George S. Patton Jr., *War as I Knew It* (Boston: Houghton Mifflin, 1947), pp.
356, 413.

The U.S. Army began World War II with a nearly nonexistent armored capability, but by astute observation and hard-won experience it eventually fielded a force that was better organized than that of its enemies or allies. By the end of the war armored forces had established a claim as a key arm in the Army's future. Having grown out of the infantry and cavalry, armor replaced the cavalry as a branch shortly after the war. The armored division underwent postwar reorganizations, but retained its flexible combat command structure until the advent of the Reorganization Objective Army Division in the early 1960s, when force designers used the combat command as a model for a new type of brigade headquarters adopted by all Army divisions.

A panzer unit sweeps across the Russian steppe during Operation BARBAROSA. The success of German armored forces early in World War II prompted a rapid search in the U.S. Army for a means to defeat this threat. *(National Archives)*

6

TANK DESTROYER FORCE

Christopher R. Gabel

The onset of World War II in Europe presented the U.S. Army with one of the starkest emergencies in its history. The armed forces of Germany, employing a new mode of warfare popularly called blitzkrieg, swept away one opponent after another. With the defeat of France in June 1940, it became increasingly likely that the United States would soon be engulfed in the war, very possibly without the assistance of allies. The U.S. Army, suffering from two decades of neglect, was not only grossly understrength but also badly out of date. Dramatic expansion and modernization would be needed before the United States could hope to confront the German menace.

The centerpiece of blitzkrieg, and the focus of concern for the U.S. Army, was the German panzer division, a highly mobile combined arms formation. A typical division at the time of the French campaign had 249 tanks, as well as motorized infantry, artillery, and supporting elements.[1] To confront this threat, the U.S. Army had only a rudimentary armored force and fielded only the weakest of antitank capabilities. The standard U.S. infantry division included just 24 obsolescent antitank guns.[2] Improvement was urgently needed.

Three individuals, starting with the Army chief of staff himself, dominated the process of innovation that produced the U.S. Army's main answer—the tank destroyer force. In April 1941 General George C. Marshall Jr. struck the first blow for innovation by assigning responsibility for antitank affairs not to one of the combat arms but to a special planning branch within the

---

[1] Karl-Heinz Freiser, *The Blitzkrieg Legend: The 1940 Campaign in the West* (Annapolis, Md.: Naval Institute Press, 2005), p. 120.

[2] Kent Roberts Greenfield, Robert R. Palmer, and Bell I Wiley, *The Organization of Ground Combat Troops,* United States Army in World War II (Washington, D.C.: Historical Division, United States Army, 1947), pp. 274–75.

War Department General Staff's G–3 division. This office evolved within a year into an autonomous Tank Destroyer Center. From there the tank destroyer force emerged, for all practical purposes, as a new combat arm within the Army's ground forces, coequal with infantry, artillery, and armor. The center, which took up residence at newly established Camp Hood, Texas, in January 1942, assumed responsibility for all individual and unit training, including its own officer candidate school. It also wrote doctrine and developed the requirements for distinctive weapons and equipment. It thus controlled all the elements needed to create an entirely new capability within the Army. By establishing the program as an independent combat arm, Marshall cut through a great deal of branch parochialism and bureaucratic inefficiency.[3]

The second key innovator was Lt. Gen. Lesley J. McNair, a senior assistant to General Marshall and later chief of Army Ground Forces, an organization established in March 1942 with responsibility for the doctrine and training of all the combat arms. "One of the most aggressive advocates of the movement to develop tank destroyers," he championed mobile tactics and the pooling of tank destroyer elements at the corps and army echelons for assignment to divisions only when and where needed.[4] The latter decision was part of his overall policy aimed at keeping the division lean and light. It would also enable tank destroyers to mass in formations up to brigade size to meet massed panzer forces on equal terms, a key element of evolving antitank doctrine.

The third and most closely involved individual was Lt. Col. (later Maj. Gen.) Andrew D. Bruce, who commanded the Tank Destroyer Center during the formative period of the program. As the key innovator in the process, Bruce shaped antitank doctrine, directed the development of tables of organization, and prescribed the type of weaponry needed to fulfill the mission. He eagerly seized the authority and latitude granted by Marshall and McNair to take the Army in an entirely new direction in the field of antitank warfare.

Bruce's tank destroyer doctrine emerged in 1942 as Field Manual (FM) 18–5, *Tank Destroyer Field Manual: Organization and Tactics of Tank Destroyer Units.* Encouraged by Marshall and McNair,

---

[3] For an account of the Tank Destroyer Center's activities, see U.S. Army, "Tank Destroyer History" (Camp Hood, Tex., [c. 1945]), Library of Congress, Washington D.C.

[4] Greenfield, Palmer, and Wiley, *Organization*, p. 74.

Bruce infused the doctrine with an aggressive, offensive spirit, as characterized by the term *tank destroyer* and by the motto "Seek, Strike, and Destroy." The hallmarks of this doctrine were mobility and firepower. Assuming that the main threat would be masses of light tanks operating at top speed, FM 18–5 posited that tank destroyers would use superior mobility to hem in the marauding tanks, maneuver against their flanks, and employ superior firepower to destroy them.[5] In Bruce's mind, tank destroyer operations assumed the character of the counterattack rather than passive defense.

To execute this ambitious doctrine, Bruce and the Tank Destroyer Center devised an equally novel organizational structure for the tank destroyer battalion, which became the building block for the entire concept. The initial version of the battalion contained a motorized reconnaissance company to find enemy armor, and three companies—each with 12 self-propelled antitank guns—to engage and destroy the opposing tanks. It also included 18 self-propelled antiaircraft guns to protect the battalion from blitzkrieg's aerial punch. A contingent of 108 security troops, also motorized, rounded out the force, for a grand total of 898 officers and men. The tank destroyer battalion could fight independently or mass into groups or even brigades when circumstances warranted.

When Bruce framed doctrine and organization in 1942, he knew the U.S. Army had no weapon that embodied the combat characteristics he had in mind. But he pushed ahead with his theoretical constructs, secure in the knowledge that he could shape procurement requirements to meet his needs. Bruce wanted a weapon system with dominant firepower and mobility, and he was willing to sacrifice armor protection to achieve that goal. Ultimately, he settled upon a design that became the M18 tank destroyer. It was a fully tracked fighting vehicle capable of 50 miles per hour on the road, with a high-velocity 76-mm. gun mounted in a fully-rotating open-topped turret. Owing to its light armor, the M18 weighed in at only 20 tons (as compared to 30 tons for the M4 Sherman tank).[6] The M18 would not, however, begin full production until well into

---

[5] See U.S. War Department Field Manual no. 18–5, *Tank Destroyer Field Manual: Organization and Tactics of Tank Destroyer Units* (Washington, D.C.: U.S. Government Printing Office, 1942).

[6] Charles M. Baily, *Faint Praise: American Tanks and Tank Destroyers During World War II* (Hamden, Conn.: Archon, 1983), pp. 48–50, 67–68.

An M6 tank destroyer. Developed as a wartime expedient, this combination 37-mm. antitank gun and 3/4-ton truck proved ineffective against German armored forces in the North Africa campaign. *(National Archives)*

1943. In the meantime, the new tank destroyer battalions would train, and even enter combat, with an assortment of improvised weapons.

The accomplishments of the three innovators—Marshall, McNair, and Bruce—were remarkable when one considers the magnitude of the innovation and the relatively short time period involved. The size of the projected tank destroyer force itself was impressive. On 7 October 1941, before the first battalion had even been activated officially, Marshall approved a planning estimate calling for a ratio of four such battalions for every division in the Army.[7] Had that goal been realized, the U.S. Army in World War II would have fielded no fewer than 360 tank destroyer battalions!

Any innovation represents a gamble. The Army attempted to mitigate the risks of this radically new antitank concept by testing a number of its precepts, in embryonic form, while the program was

---

[7] Conference in the Office of the Chief of Staff, 7 October 1941, Item 4327, Microfilm Reel 287, George C. Marshall Library, Virginia Military Institute, Lexington, Va.

in its infancy. In September and November 1941 the Army pitted its new armored divisions against experimental antitank forces in the course of the army-versus-army maneuvers held in Louisiana and the Carolinas. To be valid, any such test must be honest, impartial, and empirical. However, two shortcomings clouded the results of these experiments. First, McNair, one of the founders of the tank destroyer establishment, was also the maneuver director, leading to legitimate questions of impartiality. In truth, the umpires who adjudicated the mock battles accorded a degree of effectiveness to antitank forces that exceeded current realities. Second, by testing two experimental forces against each other, it was difficult to interpret the results. For the most part, the armored forces fell short of their objectives, but whether that was due to the effectiveness of antitank forces or to flaws within the armored establishment was a subject of debate. McNair declared that the maneuvers validated the nascent tank destroyer concept, but Armored Force commander Maj. Gen. Jacob L. Devers disagreed. He publicly declared, "We were licked by a set of umpire rules."[8] The next test of the theory would come in the heat of battle.

Seven tank destroyer battalions participated in the North African campaign that began on 8 November 1942. The results were not encouraging. It came as something of a shock when panzer divisions behaved differently than the enemy described in FM 18–5. Rather than masses of light tanks operating at top speed, the panzer divisions in Tunisia employed sophisticated combined arms teams, characterized by artillery and infantry operating in close support of the tanks, and deadly antitank fire coming from hidden overwatch positions. For the lightly armored tank destroyers, slugging it out with German tanks in the open was suicidal. It quickly emerged that the best way to meet attacking German tanks was from concealed dug-in positions—a far cry from Seek, Strike, and Destroy. This fact also doomed the idea of tank destroyers being held back in reserve, to race fire-brigade style to the scene of a German attack. If the antitank units were not on hand when the attack began, they would have to join the battle in progress and possibly have to fight exposed from a position of weakness. In any case, they were unlikely to arrive in time

---

[8] As quoted in "Second Battle of the Carolinas," *Time*, December 8, 1941, p. 66. For an analysis of the Louisiana and Carolinas exercises, see Christopher R. Gabel, *The U.S. Army GHQ Maneuvers of 1941* (Washington, D.C.: U.S. Army Center of Military History, 1992).

to retrieve the situation given the tempo of combat embodied in blitzkrieg.

Equally important, tank destroyers in North Africa operated under a handicap in regard to their equipment. Expedient weapons intended solely for training ended up fighting real panzers. The M3 Gun Motor Carriage, a 75-mm. gun mounted on a half-track, had neither superior mobility nor firepower when confronting Axis armor. The M6, an obsolete 37-mm. antitank gun mounted on a ¾-ton truck, was hopeless. The best expedient was the M10, a 3-inch gun mounted in a fully rotating open-topped turret on the chassis of an M4 Sherman tank.

Finally, the tank destroyers in North Africa discovered that the rest of the Army was largely ignorant of their doctrine, if not downright hostile to the concept they embodied. Senior commands scattered the tank destroyer battalions, attaching them out to other units in company and platoon strength and giving them missions that bore no relation to their desired methods. Opposition on the part of the Army at large was well founded, for on the rare occasions that tank destroyers did attempt to execute their primary task in accordance with theory, the results were usually costly, or disappointing, or both. A steady stream of negative reports soon flowed from North Africa to the War Department and to Camp Hood. All three men who commanded the II Corps in Tunisia—Maj. Gens. Lloyd R. Fredendall, George S. Patton Jr., and Omar N. Bradley—went on record with their disapproval of the tank destroyer concept.

Given the bad reports from Tunisia, coupled with the growing realization that Germany was losing its ability to mount great offensives, the U.S. Army began to backpedal on the tank destroyer innovation even while the war was in progress. Only 106 battalions were ever activated. Of these, 35 never left the United States, having been converted or broken up before deployment.[9] Moreover, the War Department mandated a reduction in size for the tank destroyer battalion, eliminating the antiaircraft elements and combining other functions to reduce its strength from 898 to 673 men. To address the tank destroyer doctrine's lack of credibility, Bruce and the center prepared a new field manual, published in 1944, that eliminated the word *offensive* in reference to tank destroyer tactics, downplayed the fixation on mobility, empha-

---

[9] Shelby L. Stanton, *Order of Battle: U.S. Army, World War II* (Novato, Calif.: Presidio Press, 1984), pp. 333–38.

An M10 tank destroyer dug in and camouflaged beside a haystack in Italy. From the initial offensive concept, embodied in the motto "Seek, Strike, and Destroy," the tank destroyer force devolved into a defensive organization emphasizing stealth and deception, with small units parceled out to support infantry battalions. *(U.S. Army Center of Military History)*

sized stealth and deception, and accorded more attention to the need for combined arms cooperation with the other elements on the battlefield.[10]

In yet another blow to the Seek, Strike, and Destroy doctrine, McNair himself directed in 1943 that half of all tank destroyer battalions should be converted from self-propelled to towed guns. The latter were thought to be more easily concealed. This particular measure was later reversed when experience in Europe showed the towed guns to be less effective and more vulnerable than the self-propelled models, but by that time tank destroyer doctrine was largely dead.

---

[10] See U.S. War Department Field Manual no. 18– 5, *Tactical Employment Tank Destroyer Unit* (Washington D.C.: U.S. Government Printing Office, 1944).

Starting in Tunisia and continuing through the end of the war, the tank destroyers made their greatest contributions not in the antitank role but in secondary missions, such as pillbox busting with direct fire and reinforcing field artillery with indirect fire. These missions generally entailed attaching the tank destroyers, by company, platoon, or section, to infantry or armor elements at the battalion level or lower, often on a semipermanent basis. On those increasingly rare occasions when German armor attacked in force, the tank destroyers usually fought them in small units and often from static positions. In short, little differentiated tank destroyers from the medium tanks that also served in the close-support role. At the conclusion of the war the U.S. Forces, European Theater, General Board concluded that the tank destroyer doctrine had rarely been attempted, and certainly had never been validated. The board noted that the tank destroyers were most useful in their assault gun role but that a separate tank destroyer establishment within the Army was unnecessary.[11] Shortly after the war ended, the Tank Destroyer Center ceased operations and the battalions were deactivated. Without fanfare, the tank destroyer program came to an end.

What went wrong with this innovation? In retrospect, it would appear that one key mistake was making it an independent effort. When the Tank Destroyer Center became a world unto itself, it rarely exchanged ideas with other elements of the Army (most notably the Armored Force) and ended up creating its doctrine and training its forces in isolation. Moreover, separation prevented the tank destroyer establishment from gaining acceptance from and developing a habitual relationship with the rest of the Army. When the new units arrived on the battlefields of Tunisia, they came as strangers.

Independence helped perpetuate a second mistake—flawed assumptions about the nature of armored warfare. The tank destroyer innovators assumed that blitzkrieg meant masses of tanks operating independently of the other arms. To the extent that this was ever true at all, it was sadly erroneous by 1942. The tank destroyer battalion was virtually a pure antitank force designed to meet and defeat a pure tank force. When it encountered instead a

---

[11] U.S. Forces, European Theater, General Board, "Report on Study of Organization, Equipment, and Tactical Employment of Tank Destroyer Units" [1946?], pp.10, 25, 29, Combined Arms Research Library, Fort Leavenworth, Kans.

sophisticated, mechanized, combined arms threat, it was at a distinct disadvantage. Closer interaction with the other combat arms during doctrine writing and training might have exposed some of these flawed assumptions.

Pooling tank destroyers at higher headquarters and attaching them to divisions only when needed also carried negative repercussions, for it precluded development of the habitual relationships and the combined arms training that was so essential to battlefield success. Fortunately, pooling was rarely practiced in the field, and most tank destroyer elements stayed with the same outfits for prolonged periods.

A final problem arose from the lapse of time between the emergence of embryonic tank destroyer concepts (1941) and the first contact between tank destroyers and the enemy (1943). Two years is not much time to field a completely new combat arm, but in that interval the German and Soviet armies had engaged in a furious arms race that had reshaped the nature of armored warfare. Americans in both the tank and antitank fields were only imperfectly aware of the magnitude of these developments, and were not particularly effective at forecasting trends for the near future. Specifically, in the course of combat on the Eastern Front the tank evolved from a light, mobile, blitzkrieg weapon into a massive, heavily gunned, and thickly armored antitank weapon. The M18 tank destroyer would have made mincemeat of the light Panzer IIs and IIIs that overran France in 1940, but it operated at a serious disadvantage against the German tanks that had evolved solely to kill other tanks—the Panzer V (Panther) and Panzer VI (Tiger). Only one tank destroyer model could hold its own against these opponents—the 90-mm. M36 that appeared in the last months of the war.

Conceived in haste, plagued by several bad assumptions, and handicapped by institutional isolation, the tank destroyer program fell far short of its intended goals and thus, when viewed as a case study in innovation, must be judged a failure. But through the initiative, ingenuity, and adaptive spirit of the soldiers at the front, the tank destroyers nonetheless made a significant contribution to victory in World War II, even if it was not in the manner planned by their creators.

A soldier fires a bazooka over a hedgerow in France. The man-portable rocket launcher gave infantrymen a fighting chance against enemy tanks. *(National Archives)*

7

THE BAZOOKA

Mark J. Reardon

The successful employment of German panzer divisions during the Polish and French campaigns of 1939–1940 triggered a massive effort on the part of the U.S. Army to acquire modern antiarmor weapons. At the behest of the Army Chief of Staff General George C. Marshall, junior members of the War Department staff met in April 1941 in Washington D.C. to discuss the woefully inadequate American antitank arsenal. The group, chaired by Maj. Anthony C. McAuliffe from the Office of the Chief of Logistics, evaluated a broad array of weapons capable of defeating enemy armored vehicles. The agenda included identifying a man-portable antitank weapon that could be procured quickly and in large numbers. The officers considered the feasibility of employing antitank mines, flamethrowers, smoke candles, armor-piercing rounds for heavy machine guns, and rifle grenades, and for the most part discarded them as impractical or ineffective. The lack of viable options was apparent when discussion drifted toward issuing infantrymen Molotov cocktails—field expedient weapons consisting of a gasoline-filled glass bottle with a rag for a fuse—to throw on enemy vehicles.

Lt. Col. Leslie A. Skinner and 2d Lt. Edward G. Uhl were destined to provide a solution to the dilemma facing the U.S. Army. Skinner, born in 1900 as the only son of an Army surgeon, became mesmerized during his childhood by rockets. He perfected his design and construction skills in the shop of an ordnance sergeant at Fort Strong, Massachusetts, where his father was stationed. The teenager's experiments, however, were abruptly terminated in 1915, when one of his creations set fire to the roof of the post hospital. He earned his commission from West Point in 1924 and entered the Army Air Corps, where he served as a balloon and airship pilot and air observer.[1]

---

[1] Leslie A. Skinner obituary, *Assembly*, West Point Association of Graduates 38 (September 1979): 133.

Transferring to the Ordnance Department in 1931, Skinner was initially assigned to automotive testing at Aberdeen Proving Grounds, Maryland. Inspired by a technical report on a rocket gun successfully demonstrated by Drs. Robert H. Goddard and Clarence N. Hickman on 10 November 1918, Skinner began to devote his off-duty time to developing a rocket that could be fired from an aircraft. The inquisitive officer conducted nine hundred test flights over a two-year period as he sought to translate the concept into reality.[2] Eventually his talents were used to create a one-man Army Rocket Office. He could now conduct experiments at his place of duty, but he was still limited by a very small budget.

In 1938 the Army transferred Skinner to Hawaii, but he returned two years later at the instigation of Dr. Hickman, now a member of the National Defense Research Committee. Hickman arranged for Skinner to report to the U.S. Navy Powder Factory at Indian Head, Maryland, where he was to establish an Army Special Projects Unit and continue his rocket work. Skinner soon gained an assistant, Lieutenant Uhl, a recent graduate of Lehigh University with a thorough grounding in physics and engineering.[3]

Despite Hickman's high interest, the Army rocket program remained a relatively low priority with a miniscule budget. Uhl, for example, would first search the Powder Factory's scrap heap whenever he needed some metal.[4] The nearby Potomac River served as a test firing range. Skinner frequently asked his Navy counterparts for assistance, repaying them by working on sister service projects that included rocket-guided bombs and jet-assisted takeoff.

While Skinner devoted his attention to aircraft and artillery-launched rockets, Uhl worked on an antitank design. An Ordnance Department civilian, Gregory J. Kessenich, tipped off the rocket section to the potential of a new type of explosives technology perfected by Swiss engineer Henri H. Mohaupt. In late 1940 Mohaupt had offered the U.S. Army a shaped-charge projectile. The hollow cone molded into the front of the explosive charge focused much of the blast into a hot jet that could burn a hole

---

[2] David G. Harris, "Leslie Skinner . . .: A Horn in Search of a Tune," *Army* 23 (December 1973): 34.

[3] Interv, author with Edward G. Uhl, 10 May 2006, Historians files, U.S. Army Center of Military History (CMH), Washington D.C.

[4] Interv, author with Edward G. Uhl, 18 May 2006, Historians files, CMH.

through armor. Unlike existing antitank rounds, which depended on speed and mass to create the energy to penetrate, Mohaupt's shaped charge would work even when it made contact with the target at a relatively slow speed. Thus the warhead could be fired from smaller less powerful weapons, making it perfect for use by foot soldiers.

The Ordnance Department had acquired and tested Mohaupt's 30-mm. shaped-charge rifle grenade and found it capable of penetrating 2 inches of hardened steel. Work frantically began on a 60-mm. design after the Army received a report from the British that the Germans were increasing the thickness of the armor plate on their panzers to 4 inches.[5] Standardized as the M10 grenade, the 60-mm. version was up to the new challenge, but it had gained a major flaw. The charge required to launch this heavier projectile a sufficient distance produced a great deal more recoil. Because the butt of the M1 Garand rifle had to be placed on the ground to gain elevation and range, the wooden stock absorbed the shock and often broke in the process.

In a search for something capable of launching the M10, the Army turned to a concept dubbed the spigot mortar. This notional weapon was basically a solid rod with a trigger mechanism located at the base. The projectile consisted of the shaped-charge grenade attached to a length of hollow tube that fit down over the mortar's rod. Pressing the trigger activated a firing pin located at the tip of the rod, which in turn ignited a propellant charge in the base of the grenade. The expanding gasses from the burning propellant thrust the projectile off the rod, with the tube imparting initial guidance. Similar to a traditional mortar, the recoil would be absorbed into the ground on which the weapon rested.

The advantages of the spigot mortar were several. It was small, light, easy to operate, simple to manufacture, and cheap. While the first three factors made it attractive to an infantryman, all of them were important to ordnance designers given that the Army wanted to field large numbers of the man-portable antitank system in a very short period of time. The only obvious drawback to the system was its relatively short range. The Ordnance Department asked several private firms to each develop a working spigot mortar capable of firing the 60-mm. shaped-charge grenade. The Army planned to test the prototypes in a competitive shoot off at Aberdeen in early summer 1942.

---

[5] Ibid.

While others sought ways to effectively employ the 60-mm. grenade, Uhl focused on marrying the round to a rocket that would get it to the target. By February 1942 he had successfully assembled a prototype antitank rocket by adding propellant, a gas trap, an igniter, and stabilizing fins to an inert M10 grenade. Firing tests conducted at the end of the dock that projected into the Potomac revealed that the new design had the desired range and ballistic properties. The next step was to construct a portable launcher. The main component came from an unexpected source. While rummaging through the scrap pile behind his workshop, Uhl came upon a 5-foot length of metal pipe that proved just wide enough to accept a 60-mm. round. Upon inspecting Uhl's discovery, Skinner remarked that he had a spare rifle stock at home that could be fitted to the underside of the tube. He also suggested Uhl add a pair of grips to make it even easier to handle. The pair decided to use a trigger-activated electric igniter that sent a charge through a wire to the base of the rocket.[6] Once these features were added to the design, all that remained was to conduct a live-fire test to see if everything worked.

Uhl received the mission to fire the first rocket. Wearing a welder's mask and gloves, he walked to the end of the pier. A small group of observers, including Skinner and Hickman, watched from the shore. After ensuring no watercraft were nearby, Uhl pointed the tube toward the middle of the river and pressed the trigger. When it fired, he heard only a whooshing noise and felt absolutely no recoil. He discovered that the rocket did not generate enough exhaust to justify wearing any protective equipment.

Based on this success, Uhl assembled enough inert rockets to conduct more extensive testing. Skinner decided that the combination of rocket and launcher should be tested at Aberdeen during the spigot mortar shoot off in May. On the morning of the scheduled test, Uhl and Skinner arrived at the range before anyone else. Spotting a tank in the impact area, Uhl walked over to talk to the driver who confirmed that his vehicle was indeed the target for the pending competition. The soldier also explained that he was to navigate a specific course, which he pointed out to Uhl, and that he was to do so at a speed of twenty-five miles per hour. Uhl paced off the distance back to the firing line. After scribbling some figures down on a matchbook, he concluded he had to aim one tank length in front of the vehicle and slightly

---

[6] Ibid.

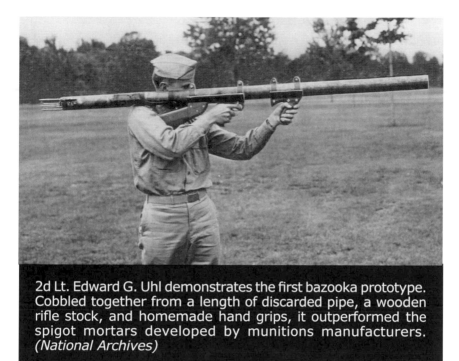

2d Lt. Edward G. Uhl demonstrates the first bazooka prototype. Cobbled together from a length of discarded pipe, a wooden rifle stock, and homemade hand grips, it outperformed the spigot mortars developed by munitions manufacturers. *(National Archives)*

above the top of the turret to obtain a hit on a moving target at that range.[7]

The crews of the spigot mortars arrived and began assembling their weapons. Uhl and Skinner occupied a sixth firing point about fifty yards to one side. A group from Army Ground Forces head-quarters, headed by a lieutenant general, appeared soon afterwards. The officers were accompanied by Brig. Gen. Gladeon M. Barnes, head of the Ordnance Department Research and Development Section.[8] The test began with a signal from Barnes to the tank crew. As the vehicle moved back and forth, the spigot mortars took turns firing dummy rounds at the target. It quickly became apparent that the high trajectory of the projectiles—required for maximizing

---

[7] Ibid.

[8] Although no records could be found that specifically identify the spigot mortars, General Barnes' weekly log indicates that the "special grenade" testing was conducted at the "trench mortar firing point." See Weekly Log, 5 Jun 1942 entry, box Activities 4/1/42 thru 6/30/42, R&D Activities: Gen Barnes, Entry 646A,Record Group (RG) 156, National Archives Records Administration–College Park (NARA–CP), College Park, Md.

range, given the low propellant charge—made the weapon highly inaccurate, especially against a moving target. Each mortar missed when its turn came, producing audible groans from onlookers.

Just before the competition began, Uhl and Skinner had realized their rocket launcher lacked a sighting mechanism. Uhl extracted a wire coat hangar and pliers from the trunk of his automobile. The young lieutenant constructed a front sight, featuring an upright blade, and a circular rear sight, in which the firer centered the front blade. Using a telephone pole as a reference point, Skinner looked down the length of the empty firing tube to ensure it remained centered on the pole as Uhl bent two sections of a coat hanger around the tube. This final modification to the launcher was completed before the spigot mortars had finished firing.

After the fifth prototype missed, Uhl took aim at the moving tank and pulled the trigger. A rocket whooshed downrange to score a direct hit. The officers sitting on the bleachers cheered and threw their hats in the air. The Army Ground Forces three-star approached Skinner to ask if he could test fire the launcher. Uhl relinquished it to the general, explaining the trigger mechanism and sighting procedures as the senior officer prepared to fire at the tank. The general scored a direct hit. Barnes now took a turn and was also successful.[9] Others test fired the weapon with only one rocket missing the target.

When all the projectiles were expended, Barnes stepped forward once more to closely examine the launch tube. He casually remarked to Skinner: "This sure looks just like Bob Burns' bazooka."[10] Burns was a famous radio comedian whose publicity photos often depicted him playing a cobbled-together musical instrument he called "The Bazooka."[11] Although the Army would formally designate the weapon the 2.36-inch rocket launcher M1, the nickname coined by Barnes would stick.

Things began moving quickly as development of the bazooka continued. A week later General Marshall and members of the Soviet and British military delegations witnessed a second demonstration held at Camp Simms in Washington D.C.[12] The Soviets

---

[9] Uhl Interv, 18 May 2006, Historians file, CMH.

[10] Ibid.

[11] Ibid.

[12] Anne J. Gregg, comp., Small Arms Div, Industrial Svc, Ord Dept, [24 Feb 1948], sub: Project Supporting Paper Relating to Rocket Launchers, World War I thru World War II (1917–August 1945), p. 9, box R&D: Ammunition Branch—Study of Commercial Type Ammunition, RG 156, NARA–CP.

were so impressed that they asked Marshall to supply them with bazookas immediately even though the weapon was still being improved. Marshall issued verbal orders that 5,000 of the rocket launchers, along with necessary quantities of rockets and practice ammunition, be produced for lend-lease purposes within a month. The General Electric plant in Bridgeport, Connecticut, learned on 20 May that it had to build the weapons as soon as possible. The company completed the initial batch of bazookas by 24 June and shipped them to the Soviet Union shortly afterwards.[13]

The Army Supply Program of 10 July 1942 set a goal of building 75,000 rocket launchers by the end of the year. With the Soviet consignment out of the way, Skinner and Uhl concentrated on getting the new weapon into the hands of American troops. Ordnance specialists made only a few changes, improving the firing mechanism, shortening the overall length by 6 inches, and placing a fixed sight at the end of the tube. Difficulties in obtaining steel tubing and production delays created by design modifications combined to limit bazooka production that month to 241 units. Most of these problems, however, were overcome within a few weeks, and more than 37,000 rocket launchers were produced for the U.S. Army by the end of October.[14]

The M1 rocket launcher first saw action with U.S. troops in November 1942 in North Africa during Operation TORCH. In the Tunisian campaign that followed, unreliable ammunition reduced the effectiveness of the bazooka. Both the rocket and the launcher had to undergo a number of improvements to make the combination a more potent weapon. In late 1943, the Army introduced the M9 version of the bazooka with a more powerful rocket—the M6A3. The Germans, based on their battle experience against Soviet tanks, were already fielding thicker and better-designed armor on new panzer models. To further counter shaped-charge warheads, they also devised additional measures that could be added to old and new tanks alike, including armored skirts that prematurely detonated incoming rockets. As a result, bazooka teams were forced to target less well-protected—and more difficult to hit— areas of enemy armored vehicles, such as tracks, suspension, or the rear engine compartment.

---

[13] Ibid, p. 10, box R&D: Ammunition Branch—Study of Commercial Type Ammunition, RG 156, NARA–CP.

[14] Ibid., app. A–2, box R&D: Ammunition Branch—Study of Commercial Type Ammunition, RG 156, NARA–CP.

Uhl holds an improved bazooka model, which was in mass production barely six weeks after the prototype demonstration. Its simplicity translated into rapid availability for troops in the field. *(National Archives)*

The Germans, who had captured copies of the early model bazooka in Russia, borrowed from Uhl's and Skinner's original design to produce their own 8.8-cm. rocket launcher. The German *Panzerfaust*—with a larger, more powerful warhead—had significantly greater armor penetration. The Americans, in turn, captured copies of the enemy rocket launcher and began designing a larger version of the M9, later designated the M20 Super Bazooka, in late 1944. However, the M20 did not see active service before World War II ended.

The reciprocal race to improve tank defenses and armor-penetrating weapons has been a feature of armored warfare since its inception. The bazooka was an innovative solution that filled a critical niche in antitank capability, but its inventors and the U.S. Army failed to foresee how rapidly the enemy would adapt to threats on the battlefield. Thus the original bazooka and subsequent improvements during the war did not keep pace with

German efforts to upgrade their panzers. Nevertheless, a number of soldiers and marines remained favorably impressed with Uhl's and Skinner's creation. It was not a foolproof tank killer, but it was the only individual weapon that gave an infantryman a fighting chance against enemy armor. Capt. Murray S. Pulver, who destroyed three panzers in Normandy, later remarked, "I always swore by the bazooka and it never let me down."[15] Fifteen American soldiers and one marine received Medals of Honor in World War II for their courage in using a bazooka against the enemy.[16]

---

[15] Interv, author with Murray S. Pulver, 12 Feb 1993, Historians files, CMH.
[16] Medal of Honor citations, Historians files, CMH.

Tracked landing vehicles (LVT) in the foreground, filled with assault troops, are preceded during a South Pacific invasion by large landing craft configured as gunboats and a line of barely visible LVT(A)4 vehicles mounting 75-mm. howitzers. The latter hit the beach first with their heavier firepower to pave the way for the infantry. *(National Archives)*

8

UPGUNNING THE AMPHIBIAN TANK

Mark J. Reardon

The invasion of Tarawa Atoll in the Central Pacific on 20 November 1943 resulted in a savage 76-hour engagement. It marked the first division-size opposed amphibious assault by U.S. forces in the Pacific, as well as the debut of the amphibian tractor in the role of assault vehicle. Ringed by coral reefs that conventional landing craft could not traverse at low tide, Tarawa presented the Americans with a special challenge from the outset. As a result, Marine planners boldly decided to use amphibian tractors, designed and built for logistical duties, to transport the first wave of troops to the beach.

While the amphibians succeeded in crossing the coral reefs, they had minimal armor protection and mounted only machine guns. Courage proved an expensive substitute for adequate armor and firepower. At least one amphibian tractor crew died when they attempted to drive up to a Japanese coast defense gun emplacement with the intention of using grenades to destroy it. Over the course of the battle, enemy fire knocked out 90 of the 2d Marine Division's 125 amphibians.[1]

Despite these high losses, employment of the amphibians reduced the human toll among the early assault echelons. Follow-on waves, carried aboard conventional landing craft, had to disembark at the reef line hundreds of yards from the beach and wade slowly ashore under heavy fire. One unit, the 1st Battalion, 8th Marines, suffered 230 killed and wounded among its 850 officers and men.[2]

The marines at Tarawa were also dependent on fire support from Navy destroyers offshore. While the latter performed admirably in most cases, the proximity of friendly troops sometimes

---

[1] Joseph H. Alexander, *Utmost Savagery: The Three Days of Tarawa* (Annapolis, Md.: Naval Institute Press, 1995), p. 232.
[2] Ibid., p. 164.

prevented the ships from engaging targets. Responsiveness also suffered because of troubles in ship-to-shore communications. While the few medium tanks available to the marines proved useful, several hours elapsed before the armored vehicles made it ashore. If the Americans wished to avoid heavy casualties at the waterline during future landings, they would have to employ more heavily armed and armored amphibians to suppress enemy defenses before the first troop carriers touched down.

The amphibians that fought at Tarawa originated from a rescue vehicle designed by Donald Roebling following a disastrous Florida hurricane in 1928. Featured in the October 1937 issue of *Life* magazine, the prototype amphibian came to the attention of Marine Corps Commandant Maj. Gen. Thomas A. Holcomb. The marines contacted Roebling, who agreed to provide them with a test model for acceptance trials. After years of experimentation, the Navy Bureau of Ships awarded a contract for 200 vehicles in February 1941, with the first amphibian tractor—or amtrac as it was more popularly known—rolling off the production line in late August.

Holcomb had asked the Bureau of Ships as early as 27 June 1941 to examine the feasibility of fielding a variant of Roebling's amphibian tractor equipped with a.50-caliber machine gun or a 37-mm. cannon, three .30-caliber machine guns, and sufficient armor to resist .30-caliber bullets, citing as the rationale for his proposal that "it would be useful for supporting infantry in the early hours of a landing."[3] Given the added capability, he specified that a design weighing up to 40,000 pounds would be acceptable.

On 9 August 1941 the Navy turned the request over to Roebling, who had recently formed a manufacturing partnership with the Food Machinery Corporation.[4] He felt that a 20-ton amphibian would not be very seaworthy and responded with a counterproposal for a 10-ton design armed with a .50- caliber and two .30-caliber machine guns.[5] Balking at the inventor's crude arrangement of the main armament, the marines suggested he go back to the

---

[3] Victor J. Croizant, *Across the Reef: The Amphibious Tractor Vehicle at War* (London: Arms and Armour Press, 1989), p. 63.

[4] By 1941 Food Machinery Corporation had established East and West Coast production sites respectively located in Lakeland, Florida, and Riverside, California.

[5] Richard W. Roan, *Roebling's Amphibian: The Origin of the Assault Amphibian* (Quantico, Va.: U.S. Marine Corps Development and Education Command, 1987), p. 35.

drawing board. In January 1942 Roebling offered up a second prototype using the turret of the Marmon Harrington ultralight tank, but he quickly scrapped it once he discovered that these vehicles were no longer being built. He then turned to a design featuring the turret of the T9E1 (later standardized as the M22) Locust airborne tank, which carried a 37-mm. gun. However, with the Locust scheduled for only limited production, he finally decided to graft a turret from the M5 Stuart light tank onto a standard amphibian tractor. The marines accepted this version.

Responding to a Joint Chiefs of Staff planning directive dated 10 June 1943, the Army also began organizing amphibian tractor units.[6] Even before the lessons of Tarawa were disseminated, the Army decided to procure armed and troop-carrying versions in approximately equal numbers. The lengthy search for a suitable turret, combined with a decision by the Navy to concentrate on producing only cargo/troop-carrying versions, delayed the combat debut of armed amphibians. Although vehicles with M5 turrets, designated as the LVT(A)1, finally began rolling off assembly lines in mid-1943, Marine and Army units did not receive any prior to Tarawa.

The first Army amphibian units were created using separate tank and armored infantry battalions already in existence. The 18th Armored Group, made up of the 2d Armored Group's Headquarters and Headquarters Company, the 708th and 773d Amphibian Tank Battalions, and the 534th and 715th Amphibian Tractor Battalions, formed at Fort Ord, California, on 27 October 1943. Fortunately for the pioneering Army amphibians, their commander was Col. William S. Triplet, an officer with a background well suited to commanding first-of-a-kind organizations.[7]

An enlisted combat veteran of World War I, Triplet graduated from West Point in 1924. He received a commission in the Infantry,

---

[6] In May 1943 the Joint Chiefs of Staff ordered the I Marine Amphibious Corps to conduct "an exhaustive test of a loaded LVT crossing coral reef[s] under heavy surf conditions." One month later the Pacific War Plans Section, Joint Planning Staff, issued Joint Planning Directive no. 205, 10 June 1943, citing "tests in the South Pacific in which amtracs 'negotiated fringing reefs in all conditions up to a 10-foot surf.'" See Alexander, *Utmost Savagery*, pp. 84–85.

[7] The 773d was later reorganized as an amphibian tractor battalion. See GO no. 13, Headquarters, XVIII Corps, Presidio of Monterey, 27 Oct 1943, and GO no. 25, Headquarters, Fourth Army, Presidio of Monterey, 26 Nov 1943, box AR [Armored] GP 18-0.1 to ARGP 18-1.13, Entry 427, Record Group (RG) 407, Records of the Adjutant General's Office, 1917–, National Archives and Records Group–College Park (NARA–CP), College Park, Md.

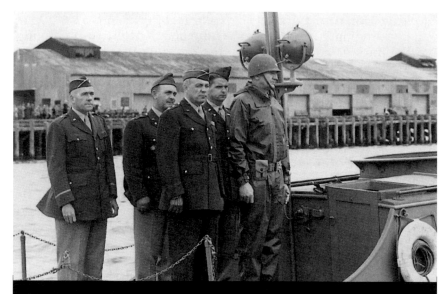

Col. William S. Triplet, wearing a helmet, commanded the Army's first amphibian unit—the 18th Armored Group. His idea to replace the 37-mm. gun and turret on the LVT(A)1 with the M8 assault gun and turret resulted in a much-improved weapon that could be fielded rapidly. *(National Archives)*

but spent much of his career working with armored vehicles. His tours included attendance at the Tank School (1929–1930), command of a company in the 2d Tank Regiment (1930–1932), and duty as a maintenance and test officer with Company F, 67th Infantry (Tanks), where he was in charge of 13 experimental vehicles (1934–1936).[8] Beginning in 1940, then Major Triplet served as a member of the Infantry Board and was involved in the development of the Jeep, the Chrysler amphibious half-ton truck, and formal evaluation of the British Bren Gun carrier.

Triplet was not afraid to explore emerging and unconventional ideas. During the late 1930s he authored (under a pseudonym) a series of popular articles in the *Infantry Journal* that chronicled the experiences of two American soldiers in a future war between the United States and the barely fictional enemy known as Munga

---

[8] William S. Triplet, *A Colonel in the Armored Divisions: A Memoir, 1941–1945*, ed. by Robert H. Ferrell (Columbia: University of Missouri Press, 2001), p. 17.

(Military Union of Germany and Asia). In these articles Triplet discussed the latest trends in doctrine and equipment by linking new military developments with the dramatic exploits of his two main protagonists—Sgts. Terry Bull (Infantry) and Horatio Bull (Tanker).[9]

While Marine counterparts fought at Tarawa, the Army's first amphibian tankers immersed themselves in the details involved in creating a new type of unit from scratch. Triplet recalled of this period: "My waking, dozing, and sleeping hours were taken up with mental arithmetic, theories of organization, training problems, and tactical uses of amphibians in combat."[10]

In early January 1944 the 18th Armored Group's subordinate battalions departed for Hawaii, while the headquarters remained behind at Fort Ord. Later that month the training cycle began anew with the arrival of the 776th Amphibian Tank Battalion and the 727th, 728th, and 536th Amphibian Tractor Battalions.[11] With reports from Tarawa available, Triplet was soon convinced that the 37-mm. gun of the LVT(A)1 would prove inadequate against Japanese bunkers and modern antitank guns. He prophesied, "My boys would be playing David versus Goliath . . . accurately throwing their shot and shell which had the explosive power of a hand grenade, until a 75-mm. shell with eight times the power tore their turret off."[12]

Triplet sent a memorandum to Army Ground Forces headquarters in Washington D.C., theorizing that if the 37-mm. Stuart turret had proven to be a successful mate to the earlier version of the LVT, then the open-topped 75-mm. howitzer turret of the M8 assault gun would work just as well. An upgunned amphibian, he argued, would not only complement "the supporting fire of destroyers, cruisers and battleships . . . [but also, once] the land tanks would be available to take over their normal role of infantry support, the amphibian tanks would [switch to providing] supporting artillery fire, using the howitzers for high-angle fire for which they were designed."[13] He concluded with a request that an "M-8 turret and howitzer be installed on an LVT(A)1 and turned over to me for a test of seaworthiness."[14]

---

[9] Idem [Terry Bull, pseud.], *Sergeant Terry Bull: His Ideas on War and Fighting in General*, Fighting Forces Series (Washington, D.C.: Infantry Journal Press, 1944).

[10] Idem, *Colonel in Armored Divisions*, p. 48.

[11] Shelby L. Stanton, *World War II Order of Battle* (New York: Galahad Books, 1991), pp. 294–95.

[12] Triplet, *Colonel in Armored Divisions*, p. 78.

[13] Ibid., p. 79.

[14] Ibid.

Triplet received a reply directing him to fasten 3,000 additional pounds—the weight difference of the heavier 75-mm. howitzer— onto an LVT(A)1; to test it in the water; and to report the results without delay. As it turned out, the heavier vehicle operated better at sea than its lighter counterpart. Triplet also received authorization to visit the Food Machinery Corporation facility at Riverside, California, to arrange for the production of a working prototype.

Three weeks later, an amtrac boasting a 75-mm. howitzer mounted in an M8 turret arrived at Triplet's headquarters. Borrowing a gunner and driver from the 776th, Triplet took the vehicle out to the group's offshore firing range. He chose not to bring a loader along because "three of us trying to fight clear in case of a [vehicle] capsize would be more than enough."[15] Once the amphibian was well out to sea, Triplet told the driver to turn off the engine and let the craft drift. He then directed the gunner to load the howitzer with a shell and full charge. After elevating the tube 10 degrees over the centerline of the hull, the first round went downrange. Although the muzzle blast was extremely loud, the discharge of the heavier weapon had minimal effect on the amphibian. It was now time to traverse the turret over the left side of the vehicle and fire another full-charge shell.

The colonel rehearsed procedures for abandoning the amphibian before instructing his gunner to "put another shell where you landed the last one."[16] The blast caused the vehicle to roll 15 degrees to the starboard (right) side before settling back down. Cranking the howitzer 180 degrees to the opposite direction, Triplet gave the command to fire just as a swell struck broadside against the amphibian. The combined action of the recoil and the wave resulted in a 25-degree roll, but the vehicle quickly settled back down.

In his report to Army Ground Forces, Triplet recommended that two-thirds of the 37-mm. vehicles in each amphibian tank company be replaced by 75-mm. variants.[17] Word of the firing tests also reached the U.S. Navy, prompting a visit from the Bureau of Ships. The naval officers were sufficiently impressed by an impromptu demonstration to order 75-mm. amphibians for the U.S. Marines.

---

[15] Ibid., p. 83.

[16] Ibid., p. 84.

[17] Amphibian tank companies now consisted of eleven 75-mm. howitzer and seven 37-mm. variants rather than eighteen of the latter. See Rpt, Co D, 776th Amphibian Tank Bn, n.d., sub: Opn STALEMATE II (Anguar Island, Pelaus), box AR [Armor] BN-776-Co(D)-0.3, Entry 427, RG 407, NARA–CP.

Soldiers rest in front of an LVT(A)4 during a lull in the fighting on Saipan in 1944. To provide additional protection against Japanese infantry, U.S. units modified these vehicles in the field with a ball-mounted machine gun visible just below the turret. *(National Archives)*

The first 75-mm. LVT(A)4 amphibians arrived in the Pacific just prior to the Marshall Islands campaign of March–April 1944. The 708th Amphibian Tank Battalion received 16, and the Marine 2d Armored Amphibian Battalion was almost entirely re-equipped. While the heavier firepower was certainly welcome, it seemed to the marines as if the new vehicle had been fielded with little thought given to the personal nature of island combat. Japanese foot soldiers, lacking advanced antiarmor weapons, such as the bazooka, frequently assaulted armored vehicles from different directions using magnetic mines or satchel charges. Multiple machine guns on every frontline armored vehicle had proven to be the only sure antidote to these close-range tactics. Amphibian tankers modified their new vehicles by replacing the .50-caliber machine gun on the open turret of howitzer-equipped models with two pintle-mounted

.30-caliber machine guns fitted with gun shields. They also added a locally fabricated ball-mounted machine gun to the front hull of each amtrac using tank bow gun components.[18]

The experiences of Capt. John A. Dean's Company A, 776th Amphibian Tank Battalion, in early December 1944 during the campaign to liberate the Philippines demonstrate the versatility and usefulness of upgunned amphibians. After being launched from a tank landing ship in Ormoc Bay, the armed amtrac company escorted troop-carrying amphibians to the beach without loss. Once ashore, one armed amtrac platoon provided on-call artillery support to the 305th Infantry while the other two platoons augmented the fires of the 902d Field Artillery Battalion.

On 9 December Company A, less one platoon that remained with the artillery, was ordered to clear a narrow strip of land between the coast road and beach in support of the 305th Infantry's advance. Dean formed his 3d Platoon into a tight wedge to spearhead the assault. Slowly grinding forward, the amtracs flattened every tree, stand of bamboo, and clump of shrubbery in their path. Despite enemy artillery fire, they moved to their objective just outside the town, outflanking and destroying several Japanese positions in the process.[19] The following morning Company A entered Ormoc ahead of its supporting infantry. The howitzer-equipped vehicles roamed the streets, firing smoke and high-explosive shells into any building suspected of harboring Japanese troops. Foot soldiers mopped up in their wake.

The next day the amtrac company relocated to the village of Lanao, where it went under control of the 77th Infantry Division's artillery and prepared for indirect fire. At 0100 on 12 December a Japanese landing ship beached nearby in an attempt to land reinforcements. Two platoons of amtracs immediately opened fire, setting the vessel ablaze and killing every enemy soldier who attempted to disembark.[20] The company remained in defensive positions near Ormoc until called upon to support another land-

---

[18] Rpt, 1st Information and Historical Service, n.d. sub: Army Amphibian and Tractor Training in the Pacific, 708th Amphibian Tank Bn; 534th, 715th, and 773d Amphibian Tractor Bns, Oct 43 to Dec 44, pp. 7–8, box ARBN-708-0.1 to ARBN-708-1.13, Entry 427, RG 407, NARA–CP.

[19] Unit History, 776th Amphibian Tank Bn, 1944, pp. 57–58, copy in U.S. Army Center of Military History (CMH), Washington D.C.

[20] Vincent P. O'Hara, *The U.S. Navy Against the Axis: Surface Combat, 1941–1945* (Annapolis, Md.: Naval Institute Press, 2007), pp. 286–87. The destroyer USS *Coghlan* also engaged the Japanese vessel.

ing on 24 December.[21] Amphibian tank units conducted similar missions time and again throughout the Pacific theater.

Triplet's brainchild, enhanced by field modifications, performed exceptionally well in combat, regardless of whether the vehicles were operated by marines or soldiers. From the moment they were first employed in the Marshall Islands, amphibian tanks mounting the 75-mm. howitzer played a useful role in the Pacific War. Without them, the island hopping campaigns that ultimately led to victory would have taken longer and cost more.

Triplet's contribution touched several levels of the innovation process. He looked ahead to see a shortcoming even before the existing equipment saw its first test in combat. Having postulated the requirement for a heavier gunned amtrac, he did not merely suggest that the Ordnance Corps develop one but came up with his own solution and convincingly argued his case. Equally important, his idea could be implemented quickly by melding existing items rather than going through the long process of designing and building a new vehicle from scratch. Finally, in his position with a training command, he was able to test the idea and prove that it worked. The Ordnance Corps generally moved slowly to upgrade weapons, preferring to gather and evaluate battlefield experience before making changes to equipment designs, production contracts, and logistical arrangements. In this case, the simplicity and effectiveness of Triplet's solution overcame the normal tendency of the bureaucracy and placed a good weapon in the hands of soldiers in a timely manner.

---

[21] Rpt, 776th Amphibian Tank Bn, n.d., sub: Opn KING II (Leyte Island), 20 Oct 44–20 Feb 45, box ARBN-776-0.3, RG 407, NARA–CP.

Tanks maneuver through hedgerow country in Normandy. Until American forces developed effective tactics and equipment, this terrain confined armored movement to narrow roads that German troops could easily defend. *(National Archives)*

9

CONQUERING THE HEDGEROWS

Mark J. Reardon

In the wake of the D-Day assault on Normandy in June 1944, American forces encountered a unique type of terrain that significantly degraded their ability to maneuver. The First Army had been aware of this obstacle for months, but had focused its planning and preparation on the amphibious landing and initial lodgment, not subsequent operations farther inland. As a result, in the midst of combat, American units had to devise new tactics, techniques, and procedures to allow them to overcome both the ground and the enemy. Known locally as the *bocage*, but commonly referred to by Americans as hedgerow country, this terrain consisted of a patchwork quilt of centuries-old interconnected hedges built up by farmers to mark the boundaries of their property, to keep in herds, and to reduce topsoil erosion by offshore winds. A typical hedgerow was three- to fifteen-feet high and consisted of earth berms crowned by a dense weave of vines, trees, and bushes. This labyrinth of narrow country lanes and natural fences extended across the width of the entire American zone of operations and inland to a depth of approximately thirty miles.

The hedgerows not only impeded tactical maneuver by American forces but also assisted the Germans, who could easily turn every pasture into a formidable fortified position. The luxuriant undergrowth also screened enemy troops from easy detection by American reconnaissance units and artillery observers. Even when U.S. soldiers could see their opponents, they experienced great difficulty identifying their own position in the confusing maze, let alone pinpointing where their targets were located. The result was a slogging yard-by-yard advance and heavy casualties.

When First Army commander Lt. Gen. Omar N. Bradley received initial reports of the difficulties encountered by his units, he gruffly commented: "Isn't this the damnedest country you ever saw? [Maj. Gen. J. Lawton] Collins says it is as bad as some of the stuff he hit on Guadal[canal]. Heavy underbrush with thick hedges. The German [takes] position under the hedges and it is necessary to root him out when he persists in sticking as he frequently does."[1] Rumors about the difficulties of hedgerow combat became so pervasive that Bradley soon asked his deputy commander, Lt. Gen. Courtney H. Hodges, to address the leaders of newly arrived units.[2] The army commander felt that a senior officer's frank discussion of the problem was the best way to educate new arrivals and to instill in them confidence in their abilities to overcome a tenacious enemy taking full advantage of the terrain.

Throughout the First Army, leaders at all echelons searched for ways to conquer the hedgerows. Rather than dictate a one-size-fits-all solution, Bradley left it to subordinate commanders to determine the best way to overcome the challenge. In turn, they settled upon a range of responses that included new tactics, improved combined arms cooperation, technological changes, modified equipment tables, or a combination of these approaches.

Maj. Henry G. Spencer, commanding the 1st Battalion, 23d Infantry, followed the path of organizational improvisation. A former enlisted marine and graduate of the Reserve Officer Training Corps at Louisiana State University, he had served with the 23d Infantry since being called to active duty. In the wake of a bloody engagement on 8 June against German paratroopers, Spencer called together his surviving officers to discuss what had taken place. One of their chief complaints centered on the relatively low number of automatic weapons in the infantry platoon. Whenever an American fired his M1 rifle, enemy paratroopers replied with a withering barrage from automatic weapons. In open terrain U.S. soldiers would have had a distinct advantage with their longer-ranged rifles, but the hedgerows frequently permitted German paratroopers armed with short-range automatic weapons to approach within yards of an American position without being detected.

After pondering the situation, Spencer asked the regiment's logistics officer, Maj. William R. Hinsch, to procure Thompson .45-caliber submachine guns from antiaircraft units protecting OMAHA beach. By the morning of 17 June the battalion's soldiers had eighty-seven additional automatic weapons. Spencer observed

---

[1] Diary, Chester B. Hansen, 19 Jun 1944, Chester B. Hansen Papers, U.S. Army Military History Institute (MHI), Carlisle Barracks, Pa.
[2] Diary, William C. Sylvan, 17 Jul 1944, William Sylvan Papers, MHI. Major Sylvan was the senior aide-de-camp for General Hodges.

that "no longer would our scouts have to go out with M1s or car-
bines to protect themselves . . . with these additional automatic
weapons; we would [now] give even the German parachutists a
run for their money."[3]

The 134th Infantry of the 35th Infantry Division was more
fortunate than most American units in Normandy because it had
a brief interval to prepare for hedgerow fighting before entering
combat. The regimental commander, Col. Butler B. Miltonberger,
was an experienced Nebraska National Guardsman. Enlisting in
1916, he saw action during World War I in the Meuse-Argonne
campaign and returned to the United States as a first sergeant.
He steadily rose in rank to assume command of the 134th in 1940.
In addition to directing each of his battalions to experiment with
the best way to attack a hedgerow, Miltonberger dispatched a
number of officers to observe the attacks on 11 July by the 134th's
sister regiments. The next day parties from both the regimental
headquarters and each rifle battalion visited elements of the com-
bat-experienced 29th and 30th Infantry Divisions to glean all the
knowledge they could.

Capt. Donald C. Rubottom, commanding Company D, 1st
Battalion, 134th Infantry, noted: "In the assembly area every
thought was directed toward the problems which might be
encountered in the fighting that lay ahead. Much had been heard
about the difficulties of fighting in the maze of hedgerows."[4] For
two days his battalion used the similar terrain around its assembly area to invent and refine special tactics. During the maneuvers
Rubottom observed that his heavy machine gunners were totally
exposed to return fire when they emplaced their tripod-mounted
weapons on top of a hedgerow. He approached the battalion's
logistics officer, 1st Lt. Robert L. Gordon, who quickly arrived at a
solution. Armorers attached bipods taken from captured weapons
to the water jackets of the heavy M1917 machine guns and the bar-
rels of the lighter M1919 models. With the flexibility to use either
mount, gunners were able to fire from behind cover and provide
more responsive support.[5]

---

[3] Henry G. Spencer, *Nineteen Days in June 1944* (Kansas City, Mo.: Lowell
Press, 1984), p. 179.

[4] Donald C. Rubottom, "The Operations of the 1st Battalion, 134th Infantry,
in the Attack on Hill 122, North of St. Lô, France, 15–17 July 1944" (Fort Benning,
Ga.: Advanced Infantry Officers Course No. 2, 1949–1950), p. 10, copy in Historians
files, U.S. Army Center of Military History (CMH), Washington D.C.

[5] Ibid, p. 11, Historians files, CMH.

In the 29th Division Maj. Gen. Charles H. Gerhardt had been learning on the job about hedgerow combat ever since splashing ashore late in the evening on 6 June 1944. A graduate of the West Point class of 1917, Gerhardt had served in France during World War I and now commanded the division. After several costly setbacks, Gerhardt instructed his assistant division commander, Brig. Gen. Norman D. Cota, to develop better tactics. Also a 1917 graduate of West Point, the 51-year-old Cota was well liked, quiet, experienced, and thoughtful. He first saw combat in World War II during the invasion of North Africa as the 1st Infantry Division's chief of staff. A natural leader who had closely supervised small-unit training prior to the invasion, Cota already had received a Distinguished Service Cross for his actions on OMAHA beach during the D-Day landings.

After some initial experimentation, Cota determined that units should be broken down into small, specialized, combined arms teams consisting of an engineer squad, one tank, and a squad of infantry reinforced by a light mortar and a machine gun. The tank initiated the assault from behind its own hedgerow, firing white phosphorous rounds to destroy machine-gun positions located in the enemy-held hedgerow. Once this process was completed, the tank began suppressing other positions along the front line while the 60-mm. mortar saturated the area behind the German position with high explosives. Under the cover of this supporting fire, infantrymen moved forward to within ten to fifteen yards of their objective and began tossing grenades. This was the signal for the tank to reverse out of position to allow the engineers to place explosive charges at the base of the friendly hedgerow. As soon as the charges detonated, the tank passed through the gap and moved on line with the infantry for the final assault against the enemy position. Given the emphasis on cross-attaching at the squad level, Cota's tactics were a significant departure from existing doctrine.[6]

Armored units initially were equally stymied by the *bocage*. Antitank guns and mines could easily dominate the narrow roads. If the tanks tried to move cross-country, they could force their way over some hedgerows but ran a significant risk when doing so because their lightly armored bellies would be exposed as they climbed over the berms. Even when tank crews were prepared to

---

[6] Michael D. Doubler, *Closing with the Enemy: How GIs fought the War in Europe, 1944–1945* (Lawrence: University Press of Kansas, 1994), pp. 54–56.

accept that risk, they discovered some hedges were so entangled with foliage and small trees that entire platoons of vehicles were immobilized while trying to bull their way through.

Surmounting the physical obstacle presented by the hedgerows rapidly became the top priority for American armored units. Sherman tanks mounting bulldozer blades proved to be a satisfactory answer, but they were such a recent development that only a few armored units were fortunate enough to possess any. The 747th Tank Battalion, which lacked any dozer-equipped tanks, developed another means to break through the barriers. Crews welded two pipes, each a few feet long and several inches in diameter, so they stuck out horizontally from the lower front of the vehicle. A tank drove the prongs into the hedgerow and then pulled back while engineers stuffed explosive charges into the holes. The resulting blast created a gap large enough for the tank to pass through.[7] The battalion soon discovered some drawbacks to this method, as the explosion alerted the defenders to the location of the attack, and it proved to be a slow process when trying to maneuver a large force of tanks through the never-ending succession of berms.

On 9 July 1944 V Corps commander Maj. Gen. Leonard T. Gerow asked Maj. Arthur C. Person of the 102d Cavalry Reconnaissance Squadron for ideas. In turn, the squadron's light tank company commander, Capt. James G. Depew, convened a meeting of his officers and sergeants to brainstorm possible solutions. One section leader, Sgt. Curtis G. Culin III, suggested that if metal teeth were mounted on the light tanks, the vehicles would be able to chew their way through the hedgerows. Depew took Culin to the squadron maintenance officer, Capt. Stephen M. Litton, to discuss the concept in greater detail. Convinced their idea had merit, Litton dispatched a team to OMAHA beach to salvage German anti-invasion obstacles. Returning with a load of scrap angle iron, three of Litton's mechanics—T/5 John Jessen, T/5 Ernest Hardcastle, and T/4 Wesley A. Hewitt—worked into the night cutting and welding.[8] Two days later Depew informed his squadron executive officer, Maj. George S.

---

[7] AAR, 747th Tank Bn, Jul 1944, box AR [Armor] BN-747-0.1 to ARBN-747-0.3, Entry 427, Record Group (RG) 407, Records of the Adjutant General's Office, 1917–, National Archives and Records Administration–College Park (NARA–CP), College Park, Md.

[8] Combat History, 10 Jun 1944 to 8 May 1945, 102d Cav Recon Sqdn, Mech, p. 3, box AV-102-0.1, Entry 427, RG 407, NARA–CP.

Sgt. Curtis G. Culin III developed one field expedient solution to the hedgerow problem. His idea of creating teethlike cutters using steel salvaged from German beach obstacles proved effective in permitting tanks to break through the earthen berms. *(National Archives)*

Saunders, that he had a working prototype.[9]

The cavalrymen tried the device and the prongs fulfilled their promise, slicing into the lower portion of the berm and loosening the packed dirt so that the tank could push through. At least one other unit was pursuing a similar solution. Company H, 66th Armor, 2d Armored Division, installed rudimentary cutters on two tanks in each platoon in late June.[10] Subsequent testing of Culin's version showed that Sherman tanks so equipped could now easily smash through all obstacles in the *bocage*, while the smaller M5 Stuart light tanks were able to break a hole in most but not all hedgerows. As Culin remarked in a postwar interview, "You'll just have to call it a field expediency. . . . The Germans had constructed road blocks of half-inch angle iron and it seemed to me something could be done about using the stuff to prod into the hedgerows. We tried using them in various ways. Finally, we took four pieces, each about three feet long, had them welded to a plate and bolted the contrivance to the front shackles of a tank."[11]

Culin's invention quickly attracted the attention of General Bradley, who attended a demonstration in mid-July. Recognizing

---

[9] W. L. White, "Sergeant Culin Licks the Hedgerows," *Readers Digest,* February 1950, p. 83.

[10] Gordon A. Blaker, *Iron Knights: The United States 66th Armored Regiment* (Shippensburg, Pa.: Burd Street Press, 1999), p. 228.

[11] *St. Louis Post Dispatch,* 2 Jul 1945.

the potentially significant tactical benefits offered by the contrivance, Bradley ordered the First Army's Ordnance Section to
assemble as many of the devices as possible.[12] Using metal taken
from German beach obstacles, soldiers constructed more than
500 devices in eleven days, with priority going to armored units
slated for the VII Corps assault codenamed Operation COBRA. The
2d Armored Division asked for and received over 250 hedgerow
cutters; the 3d Armored Division obtained only 57 modified versions, known as Douglas Cutters; and the separate armored battalions supporting the 1st, 4th, and 30th Infantry Divisions got the
remainder, which proved sufficient to equip virtually every tank
in those units.

The 2d Armored Division, the more experienced of the two
armored divisions designated to take part in the COBRA offensive, did not confine its preparations to acquiring hedgerow cutters. Between 19 and 25 July its Combat Command A conducted
a series of exercises aimed at improving tank-infantry cooperation with the attached 22d Infantry. The foot soldiers spent several
days learning how to execute the new tactics with the modified
medium tanks.[13]

Culin, who survived Normandy but lost his left leg to a land
mine in Germany in November 1944, eventually received a Legion
of Merit for his invention. After the war, General of the Army
Dwight D. Eisenhower said Culin's forklike device "saved 10,000
American lives."[14] In fact, the cutters did not always work out as
envisioned, in part because the situation changed. The steel prongs
protruding several feet in front of the tank actually impeded
vehicular movement in terrain heavily cratered by pre-COBRA sat-
uration bombing. Fortunately, the aerial bombardment had also
severely disorganized the German panzer division sitting astride
the planned VII Corps axis of advance, permitting the Americans
in many cases to advance quickly, sometimes by lightly defended
roads, rather than fight their way through the hedgerows one field
at a time. But a V Corps supporting attack conducted by the 2d
Infantry Division on 26 July demonstrated that the Culin device
worked as anticipated. The division's 9th Infantry, aided by tanks

---

[12] J. Lawton Collins, *Lightning Joe: An Autobiography* (Novato, Calif.: Presidio
Press, 1994), p. 236.

[13] George F. Wilson, *If You Survive: From Normandy to the Battle of the Bulge to
the End of World War II—One American Officer's Riveting True Story* (New York: Ivy
Books, 1987), pp. 13–14.

[14] *St. Louis Post Dispatch*, 2 Jul 1945.

A Sherman tank plows through a hedgerow. The cutters are visible underneath the dirt heaped on them at the front of the tank. *(National Archives)*

fitted with hedgerow cutters, advanced almost five miles against obstinate resistance over a two-day period.[15]

The ad hoc process by which American units arrived at solutions to the challenges presented by the hedgerows reveals both strengths and weaknesses. With VII Corps perhaps the sole exception, systematic dissemination of newly developed tactics and technology lagged significantly or did not occur at all. Success depended largely upon the initiative and competence of individuals at all levels of command. If a unit's leadership failed to find an effective alternative, it suffered heavy losses with little or no gain. The 749th Tank Battalion, operating in support of the 79th Infantry Division, reported in late July that it continued to receive

---

[15] *Combat History of the Second Infantry Division in World War II*, n.d., pp. 36–37, copy in CMH.

"extremely poor cooperation by supporting infantry."[16] That contrasts sharply with the sophisticated combined arms tactics developed by the 2d Armored Division and 29th Infantry Division.

One benefit to the diffuse improvisation effort was the wide range of minds working on the issue and developing a menu of solutions. Ultimately, the mix of hedgerow-busting tactics, technology, and teamwork adopted by individual units allowed the First Army to conduct sustained offensive operations prior to launching a decisive breakout attempt in late July. But the failure of higher headquarters to proactively examine the problems of fighting in the *bocage* meant that junior officers and soldiers had to learn the hard way in the midst of battle and suffer heavy losses in men and material in the process. Had they not exhibited tremendous ingenuity and personal initiative during this period, the American experience in Normandy might have turned out far differently.

---

[16] AAR, Co A, 749th Tank Bn, Jul 1944, box ARBN-749-0.1 to ARBN-749-3.2, Entry 427, RG 407, NARA–CP.

Soldiers of the 7th Infantry Division in their forward trench line. A combination of manpower problems and the static nature of the Korean War beginning in mid-1951 made it difficult for the Army to develop infantrymen skilled in patrolling. *(National Archives)*

10

SPECIAL PATROL GROUPS

William M. Donnelly

The U.S. Army has a long history of creating ad hoc elite formations, usually when commanders faced difficult situations that
they believed were beyond the ability of the average infantryman. These conditions arose from the nature of the conflict, such
as unconventional combat in the Indian Wars or the Philippine
Insurrection; the nature of the battlefield, in the form of formidable terrain or enemy defenses, an example being the World War
II campaign in Italy; or the limitations of available manpower due
to personnel turnover, insufficient training, or similar issues. The
senior leaders formed these elite units by placing some of their
best soldiers—men possessing a high degree of skill in field craft
and weapons, along with a high level of initiative and desire for
action—in special groups under carefully selected leaders to conduct operations whose successful execution required uncommon
talents.[1] During the Korean War's last two years, many commanders faced similar problems and often turned to ad hoc elites as a
solution.

The nature of the conflict and the battlefield in Korea changed
as negotiations began in July 1951, and the Eighth Army shifted
from a war of movement to a linear defense of the United Nations
front centered on the main line of resistance. This extensive system
of field fortifications tracing steep hills and ridges was mirrored
along the enemy's front lines. To control the area in between, U.N.
forces over the winter of 1951–1952 developed the outpost line
of resistance, a system of squad to company-size fortified points
on key terrain. Many of the most intense combat actions during
1952–1953 involved the defense of outposts against Communist
attacks.

---

[1] Andrew J. Birtle, *U.S. Army Counterinsurgency and Contingency Operations
Doctrine, 1860–1941* (Washington, D.C.: U.S. Army Center of Military History,
1998), pp. 43–47, 74–76, 116, 165–66, 225.

Although the overall campaign was static in nature, American units patrolled extensively, day and night, in groups from a few men to a reinforced rifle company. These small-unit operations provided security and early warning for both outposts and the main front line, gained intelligence and denied it to the enemy, raided Communist positions to capture prisoners and destroy fortifications, and promoted an aggressive spirit among infantrymen. This last objective was the most important for some commanders, as they feared that the skill and discipline of infantry units would erode if they remained fixed in trenches and bunkers.[2]

Senior officers also sought to "retain the sharpness of our willingness to keep fighting" by stressing the importance of capturing prisoners.[3] Eighth Army's stated reason was the need to gather intelligence, but, as contemporary critics of this policy pointed out, other sources often provided more timely information at a lesser cost. The pressure to capture prisoners could become quite intense. Eighth Army's June 1952 directive that divisions would capture one prisoner every three days led British 1st Commonwealth Division commander Maj. Gen. A. J. H. Cassels to protest. He noted that meeting that objective in I Corps had "given the enemy eight times as many PW [prisoners of war] as we have got from him."[4]

Although the nature of the war made patrolling a primary tactic, standard units found it difficult to perform this mission

---

[2] Discussion of the Eighth Army's active defense is based on Walter G. Hermes, *Truce Tent and Fighting Front*, United States Army in the Korean War (Washington, D.C.: Office of the Chief of Military History, Department of the Army, 1966); Norman W. Hicks, "U.S. Marine Operations in Korea, 1952–1953, with Special Emphasis on Outpost Warfare" (M.A. thesis, University of Maryland, 1962); contemporary articles in *Infantry School Quarterly* and *Combat Forces Journal*; monthly command reports of infantry regiments in Korea from July 1951 to July 1953, in Command Reports (Cmd Rpts), 1949–1954, Entry NM3 429, Record Group (RG) 407, Records of the Adjutant General's Office, National Archives and Records Administration–College Park (NARA–CP), College Park, Md.; and Maj Gen Lionel C. McGarr, "Personal Observations on Korean Operations," 10 May 1954, box 100, Entry A1 2, RG 550, Records of the United States Army, Pacific, NARA–CP.
[3] Ltr of Instruction no. 11 (quoted words), 23d Inf, 22 Dec 1951, copy in Cmd Rpt, Dec 1951, 23d Inf, box 2703, RG 407, NARA–CP.
[4] Cmd Rpt, Jan 1952, 9th Inf, box 2829; Cmd Rpt, Jun 1952, 14th Inf, box 3934; and Cmd Rpt, Jan 1953, 31st Inf, box 3390. All in RG 407, NARA–CP. See also Ltr (quoted words), Maj Gen A. J. H. Cassels, Cdr, 1st Commonwealth Div, to Gen James A. Van Fleet, 8 Jul 1952, file 7, box 68, James A. Van Fleet Papers, George C. Marshall Library, Lexington, Va.; McGarr, "Personal Observations on Korean Operations," 10 May 1954, box 100, RG 550, NARA–CP.

effectively for a number of reasons. Political decisions to limit war aims and national mobilization caused many American infantrymen to question the need to risk their lives in Korea. Policies limiting the length of service of draftees and reservists also created extensive personnel turbulence, placed a heavy burden on the training system, and prevented units from building a cadre of experienced specialists and leaders. Implementation of a rotation policy for individuals in Korea in early 1951 exacerbated these problems, because a typical infantryman would serve for only nine to ten months at most. The Army's inability to provide units with sufficient replacements led to an expansion of the Korean Augmentation to the U.S. Army (KATUSA) program. Most rifle squads, authorized nine men, had two or three Koreans by late 1952. The resulting language and cultural barriers further reduced unit effectiveness.[5]

In this environment commanders went to great lengths to raise the quality of infantry in Korea. When battalions were not on the front line, they engaged in training programs that stressed patrolling, night operations, and squad and platoon tactics. Divisions and regiments established replacement training programs, designed to introduce new men to combat conditions in Korea, as well as schools in such subjects as leadership, patrolling, and calling for indirect fire. These efforts helped, but they were insufficient to overcome systemic difficulties and raise the overall quality of infantry units to a high level.[6]

During World War II a number of Army divisions and regiments had pooled some of their best infantrymen into temporary outfits dedicated to patrolling. This adaptation received attention in observer reports and professional journals, but postwar doctrine did not endorse it. Indeed, the Army shelved the idea of elite infantry completely when it did away with ranger battalions and

---

[5] William M. Donnelly, "'The Best Army That Can Be Put in the Field in the Circumstances': The U.S. Army, July 1951–July 1953," *Journal of Military History* 71 (July 2007): 809–47.

[6] See regimental Cmd Rpts, RG 407, NARA–CP; Army Field Forces Observer Team Rpts no. 6 (Feb–Mar 52), no. 7 (Oct–Nov 52), and no. 8 (Apr–May 53), box 88, Entry NM 51, RG 337, Records of Headquarters, Army Ground Forces, NARA–CP; Comments, Lt Gen Reuben E. Jenkins, 6 Oct 1953, sub: Operations in Korea, box 292, Entry A-1 548, RG 338, Records of U.S. Army Operational, Tactical, and Support Organizations (World War II and Thereafter), NARA–CP; McGarr, "Personal Observations on Korean Operations," 10 May 1954, box 100, RG 550, NARA–CP.

their training programs. For a brief time ranger companies reappeared in Korea, but that experiment ended in July 1951 due to confusion over their proper role, the traditional institutional Army distaste for elite units, and the belief of many senior officers that such organizations skimmed off the best men from line infantry units. The ranger training program at Fort Benning, Georgia, survived as a means to create a cadre of noncommissioned officers (NCO) that would infuse such skill and aggressiveness into regular units, but the program never worked because too few NCOs volunteered.[7]

At the same time the ranger companies disappeared in Korea, some American commanders concluded that average infantrymen were not likely to attain the skills and inclination needed to wage a war of patrols and raids. One such leader was Maj. Gen. John W. O'Daniel, who took command of the I Corps in July 1951. His analysis of the situation led him back to the same solution he had used seven years earlier as a division commander at Anzio—a battle patrol composed of selected volunteers who would receive special training. While this outfit would not relieve line units of all patrolling responsibilities, it would provide an elite body to take on the most difficult missions, particularly capturing enemy prisoners.[8]

The corps commander began with his former World War II unit, the 3d Infantry Division. On 23 July its regiments received orders to improve their patrolling performance, primarily by establishing a battle patrol "comprised of volunteers only, designed particularly for capturing prisoners. This unit should be trained just as hard and as thoroughly as any Ranger company is trained."[9] The directive did not set a fixed structure. The 15th Infantry established its battle patrol by 1 August. The unit consisted of a five-man headquarters and four squads of six men each. To be selected

---

[7] David W. Hogan, *Raiders or Elite Infantry? The Changing Role of the U.S. Army Rangers from Dieppe to Grenada* (Westport, Conn.: Greenwood Press, 1992), pp.105–42; Memo, Office of Chief, Army Field Forces (CofAFF) for Asst Chief of Staff, G–3, DA, 13 Feb 1953, sub: Ranger Training for Leader's Course Graduates, box 26, Entry NM5 55D, RG 337, NARA–CP; "From the Schools," *Combat Forces Journal* 3 (May 1953): 40.

[8] Training (Tng) Memo no. 5, I Corps, 23 Jul 1951, and Ltr of Instruction, I Corps, 22 Jul 1951, copies in G–3 Jnl, Cmd Rpt, Jul 1951, I Corps, box 1549; Combat Bull no. 11, I Corps, 21 Aug 1951, copy in G–3 Jrl, Cmd Rpt, Aug 1951, I Corps, box 1555. Both in RG 407, NARA–CP.

[9] Min, 3d Inf Div, 23 Jul 1951, sub: Commanders' Meeting, copy in Cmd Rpt, Jul 1951, 3d Inf Div, box 2906, RG 407, NARA–CP.

Men of the 3d Ranger Infantry Company adjust their gear before undertaking a dawn patrol across the Imjin River in April 1951. Ranger units disappeared from the Army soon after, and commands in Korea began developing alternatives to re-create that capability. *(National Archives)*

for the unit, individuals had to be "adept at scouting and patrolling and possessing an inherent desire to close with and destroy or capture the enemy." The unit would operate under the control of the regiment's operations officer, but training was the responsibility of the battle patrol leader. Its members would be excused from all normal fatigue duties.[10]

Most of the other U.S. Army regiments in I Corps soon established their own special patrol groups. These provisional outfits

---

[10] Tng Memo no. 12, 3d Inf Div, 1 Aug 51, copy in G–3 files, Cmd Rpt, Aug 1951, 3d Inf Div, box 2914; Memo (quoted words), 15th Inf, 28 Jul 1951, sub: 15th Infantry Regiment Battle Patrol, copy in Cmd Rpt, 15th Inf, Jul 1951, box 2956, RG 407, NARA–CP.

shared the same characteristics of the 3d Infantry Division's battle patrols—volunteers led by specially selected officers and NCOs, armed mainly with automatic weapons, given privileges and intensive training, and reserved for more difficult missions. Organizational details varied. The 27th and 35th Infantry regiments both formed a special patrol platoon, while the 24th Infantry and 7th Cavalry regiments ordained one such platoon for each of their battalions. The 27th's Wolfhound Raiders had three seven-man squads and a two-man headquarters, while the 35th's Cacti Raiders had four seven-man squads and a six-man headquarters. The 24th's battalion special patrols consisted of one officer and a minimum of thirty enlisted men, and the 7th's battalion raider elements were squad size. Control over the special units varied; some regiments placed them under the operations officer and others under the intelligence officer. During the remainder of 1951 the practice of establishing a special patrol group did not spread much beyond I Corps, with only the 24th Infantry Division's 21st Infantry following suit.[11]

Each group received somewhat different training, relying primarily on the combat experience and imagination of members, as no official doctrine existed for this type of unit. Often the outfits emulated ranger training, which was not surprising given the similarity of missions and the presence in some groups of former rangers. Preparation focused on physical conditioning, individual and unit movement techniques, battle drills, planning for raids and ambushes, hand-to-hand combat, weapons use and maintenance, land navigation, first aid, communications equipment and procedures, adjusting indirect fire, enemy weapons and tactics, handling prisoners, and reporting information. Because most missions were to take place under cover of darkness, night operations received emphasis.[12]

---

[11] Memo, 27th Inf, 14 Aug 51, copy in Cmd Rpt, Aug 1951, 27th Inf, box 3855; Tng Memo, 24th Inf, 19 Aug 1951, in Cmd Rpt, Aug 1951, 24th Inf, box 3846; Memo, 35th Inf, 15 Aug 51, in Cmd Rpt, Aug 1951, 35th Inf, box 3866; Cmd Rpt, Aug 1951, 7th Cav, box 4511; Cmd Rpt, Dec 1951, 21st Inf, box 3675. All in RG 407, NARA–CP. See also Lt. William C. Kimball, "We Need Intelligence and *Raider* Platoons," *Infantry School Quarterly* 42 (January 1953): 42–50.

[12] David H. Hackworth and Julie Sherman, *About Face: The Odyssey of an American Warrior* (New York: Simon and Schuster, 1989), pp. 144–52; Kimball, "We Need Intelligence and *Raider* Platoons," pp. 42–50. See also Cmd Rpt, Aug 1951, 24th Inf, box 3846; Cmd Rpt, Dec 1951, 21st Inf, box 3675; Cmd Rpt, Aug 1951, 35th Inf, box 3866; and Memo, 15th Inf, 28 Jul 1951, sub:15th Infantry Regiment Battle Patrol, copy in Cmd Rpt, Jul 1951, box 2956. All in RG 407, NARA–CP.

Generally, the special units conducted a mission every three to seven days, using the time between to recover, train, and plan the next operation. The size of the element used on missions varied from teams of four or five men to the entire patrol group, depending on the task and the tactical inclination of the group's leader. Inevitably the outfits also came to be used as a handy pocket reserve force handling more-routine missions. In September and October 1951, for instance, the 15th Infantry's battle patrol spent much of its time providing security for the regiment's heavy mortar company, which had displaced forward of the front line to support a patrol base.[13]

Of the thirty-seven special patrol group actions identified in the period August–December 1951, twenty-two resulted in some type of contact with the enemy. The Americans initiated seventeen of the contacts. Total casualties among the ad hoc elite were nine dead, forty-five wounded, and one missing. Most of these casualties came from one action. In November the 27th Infantry's unit was surprised during a raid on Hill 400 when the Chinese quickly reinforced their outpost. The Americans drove off the counterattack, but at the cost of seven dead and thirty-one wounded. Communist casualties during the various actions were undetermined, though in several cases it is clear that American firepower inflicted significant losses. The special patrol groups, however, were not as successful at one of the primary missions: They took only one prisoner who lived to be interrogated.[14]

During 1951 only a few units recorded an evaluation of special patrol group performance. The 2d Battalion, 24th Infantry's Spearhead Raiders had not taken any prisoners, but they had brought back "some valuable information." The 21st Infantry's Gimlet Grenadiers "performed their assigned missions in an excellent manner. Their training in night operations and closely coordinated platoon operations enabled them to strike swiftly, inflict heavy casualties on the enemy, and return with a minimum number of casualties within the platoon."[15]

---

[13] Cmd Rpts, Sep–Dec 1051, 15th Inf, boxes 2957–59; Cmd Rpts, Sep–Oct 51, 35th Inf, boxes 3867–68. All in RG 407, NARA–CP.

[14] See Cmd Rpts, Aug–Dec 51, 7th, 15th, 21st, 27th, and 35th Inf, RG 407, NARA–CP. See also Kimball, "We Need Intelligence and *Raider* Platoons," pp. 42–50; Hackworth and Sherman, *About Face*, pp. 178–89.

[15] S–2 Rpt (quoted words), Aug 51, 2d Bn, 24th Inf, in Cmd Rpt, Aug 1951, 24th Inf, box 3846; Annex A to Cmd Rpt (quotation), Dec 1951, 21st Inf, box 3675. Both in RG 407, NARA–CP.

The 35th Infantry evidently found its Cacti Rangers to be unnecessary, and it disbanded the platoon in early November. Other special patrol groups survived into 1952, but not for long. Most disappeared without any explanation in the records. Battle patrols in the 3d Infantry Division lasted until spring 1952, when each regiment disbanded them during a lengthy period in reserve. One reason may have been that they were too expensive to maintain, given the continual shortage of high-quality leaders and the extensive personnel turbulence created by rotation. In February 1952 the 7th Infantry's commander complained that provisional units took too many men away from the line companies at a time when the regiment also had to operate a training center because of deficiencies in the replacements being received.[16]

While special patrol groups in I Corps did not last long into 1952, other units turned to similar ad hoc elites that same year in an attempt to deal with the same difficulties. This second wave of provisional outfits came not in response to a higher directive, however, but in the form of independent initiative by lower-level commanders.

Failure to meet quotas for enemy prisoners led to the first appearance of special patrol groups in the 2d Infantry Division. In January each battalion of the 23d Infantry organized squad-size special raiding patrols comprised of one officer and nine enlisted men, all handpicked volunteers. These groups had five days of training in the rear area before beginning operations. During the month, however, the special patrols took no prisoners. When the regiment entered a two-month period in reserve in the spring, the special units disappeared. Extensive personnel turnover may have been the cause. In April–June 1952 the regiment received 1,460 replacements, which undoubtedly involved a loss of many experienced leaders and likewise required a focus on basic squad-level training.[17]

In the 9th Infantry special patrol groups first appeared in February in the 3d Battalion, a month after Lt. Col. Robert W. Garrett took command. Garrett, who had commanded the 6th Ranger Battalion during World War II, organized a ranger platoon

---

[16] Cmd Rpt, Nov 1951, 35th Inf, box 3869, RG 407, NARA–CP; Hackworth and Sherman, *About Face*, pp. 196–98.
[17] Cmd Rpts, Jan–Jun 1952, 23d Inf, boxes 2835–38, RG 407, NARA–CP; Tng Memo no. 3, CofAFF, 18 Feb 1952, sub: Ranger Training, file 353, box 527, Entry A1 132, RG 338, NARA–CP

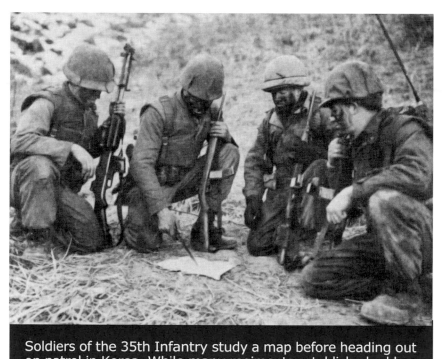

Soldiers of the 35th Infantry study a map before heading out on patrol in Korea. While many regiments established ad hoc organizations dedicated to patrolling, none of these special units proved effective enough to remain in existence for long. *(National Archives)*

in his new unit. The platoon ran its first patrol on 29 February, and in March did nine of the nineteen patrols conducted by the battalion. The regiment's 2d Battalion soon followed this lead. The 9th Infantry spent May and June in reserve and received 1,537 enlisted replacements. The commanders of both 2d and 3d Battalions also transferred to other billets. As in the 23d Infantry, the 9th Infantry special patrol groups did not survive this period off the front line.[18]

Two regiments of the 45th Infantry Division turned to special patrol groups. Both outfits formed their units from ranger-trained personnel, though each took a different approach. The 179th Infantry organized one patrol group in each battalion, with the specific structure left to the battalion commander. The 279th

---

[18] Cmd Rpts, Jan–Jun 1952, 9th Inf, boxes 2829–2831, RG 407, NARA–CP.

Infantry organized a 32-man regimental raider platoon under a lieutenant who had served in the 10th Ranger Company.[19] The 179th and 279th raiders performed well in March and April, but were disbanded in May. The division commander, Maj. Gen. James C. Styron, was never a champion of ad hoc elites, writing in early April: "[I]t is now believed that all line infantry units should be proficient in patrolling, and the formation of special units for this purpose is unnecessary." The 279th Infantry's commander, Col. P. J. C. Murphy agreed, writing also in early April that while "the Raider Platoon is considered valuable for special missions, it is now felt that normal infantry platoons with proper help from the Battalion and Regimental Staff can be equally effective."[20]

Over the course of the next several months, special patrol groups appeared in six other infantry regiments—the 9th, 15th, 23d, 31st, 32d, and 38th. They often were dubbed raiders or rangers and sometimes bore the name of the battalion or regimental commander who established them. They had mixed results, in some cases conducting a high proportion of the parent outfit's patrols or making the most contacts and occasionally suffering high casualties that generally were not justified by the results obtained. In all cases they disappeared when their patron departed or when the regiment spent a lengthy period in reserve.[21]

Little use appears to have been made of special patrol groups during 1953. One reason may have been the challenge of finding enough of the raw material needed for such units—experienced, proficient, and aggressive infantrymen. As the South Korean Army expanded, it took over more of the front line, thus limiting

---

[19] William M. Donnelly, "Under Army Orders: The U.S. Army National Guard During the Korean War" (Ph.D. diss., Ohio State University, 1998), ch. 5; William Berebitsky, *A Very Long Weekend: The Army National Guard in Korea, 1950–1953* (Shippensburg, Pa.: White Mane Publishing, 1996), pp. 166–67. See also Cmd Rpt, Feb 1952, 179th Inf, box 4339; Cmd Rpt, Feb 1952, 279th Inf, box 4347; Cmd Rpt, Mar 1952, 179th Inf, box 4339; and Cmd Rpt, Mar 1952, 279th Inf, box 4348. All in RG 407, NARA–CP.

[20] Cmd Rpts, Apr–May 1952, 179th Inf, box 4341; ibid., Apr–May 1952, 279th Inf, boxes 4348–49; Ltr (first quotation), Maj Gen James C. Styron, Apr 1952, End to Cmd Rpt (second quotation), Mar 1952, box 4348. All in RG 407, NARA–CP.

[21] See Cmd Rpts, Aug–Dec 1952, 9th Inf, boxes 2832–34; Cmd Rpt, Mar 1952, 15th Inf, box 3036; Cmd Rpts, Sep–Dec 1952, 23d Inf, boxes 2839–41; Cmd Rpts, Jun–Aug 52, 31st Inf, boxes 3340–43; Cmd Rpts, Sep–Dec 1952, 38th Inf, boxes 2851–55. All in RG 407, NARA–CP. See also ibid., Jul and Aug 1952, 32d Inf, box 313, RG 338, NARA–CP; Joseph R. May, *The Second United States Infantry Division in Korea, 1951–1952* (Tokyo: Toppan Printing Co., 1953), pp. 61–62.

the opportunities for American soldiers to gain combat experience. Inadequate preparation of soldiers in the United States persisted, with Army Field Forces noting in April that reports from Korea "continue to indicate training deficiencies in patrolling and night operations." Finally, Eighth Army—reflecting the concern over casualties back in the United States—discouraged aggressive action by American units and directed commanders "to make every effort to reduce combat losses to an absolute minimum."[22]

Special patrol groups established in Korea during the war's last two years proved to be sometimes powerful yet brittle instruments for battalion and regimental commanders. With properly selected soldiers and leaders, these ad hoc elites became highly skilled units able and willing to conduct high-risk missions beyond the capability of average infantry units. Under the commander's direct control, the special formations could be used to shape his portion of the battlefield by gathering intelligence, disrupting enemy patrolling, and meeting the demand for prisoners. Their small size and select nature, however, made them vulnerable to the pressures of personnel rotation and a single engagement resulting in mass casualties. Also, their elite status did little or nothing to fulfill one of the stated rationales behind the patrolling campaign—to maintain or enhance the fighting spirit and combat edge of infantry units defending fixed positions. The fate of these ad hoc elites suggests that their greatest weakness was their dependence on the commanders who created them. The special patrol groups existed outside of formal tables of organization, and thus the loss of the respective patron's confidence and/ or his departure from the parent command usually meant quick dissolution.

That these formations appeared and reappeared says much about the frustrations during this period of the war for senior Army infantry commanders. Constrained by the nation's war aims and strategy, they searched for methods with which they could aggressively engage the enemy in accordance with their training, experience, and inclination. Left to their own devices to solve problems arising from issues beyond their control, frontline leaders mostly came up with slight variations on the same theme of small

---

[22] Memo, CofAFF, 28 Apr 1953, sub: Emphasis in Training, box 721, Entry NM5 56, RG 337; Memo, Eighth US Army in Korea, 12 Dec 1952, sub: Conduct of Operations, file 370, box 833, Entry A1 133, RG 338; Cmd Rpts, Mar and May 1953, 27th Inf, boxes 3977–78, RG 407. All in NARA–CP.

elite units. That most groups lasted only a few months and none remained at the armistice indicates that this widespread attempt at innovation ultimately did not achieve the desired result.

The special patrol groups likely never fulfilled their purpose in large measure because the logic behind them was flawed. If the main rationales for patrolling were to maintain the aggressiveness of the army and make up for insufficiently trained and experienced manpower, reliance on an elite proved to be a veneer that did nothing to fix the underlying shortcomings throughout the force. In fact, it exacerbated both difficulties because regular units gave up many of their best infantrymen and turned over most patrolling missions to the special groups. Frontline innovation in this case proved ineffective, although the effort failed precisely because the problems were due to high-level policies that simply could not be overcome by any local initiative.

Helicopters of the 1st Cavalry Division (Airmobile) deliver a second wave of troops to a landing zone during Operation PERSHING in 1967. Developed for a nuclear conflict, the airmobile concept proved valuable during the war in Vietnam. *(U.S. Army Center of Military History)*

11

AIRMOBILITY

Mark D. Sherry

One of the most significant operational innovations during the last half of the twentieth century was the harnessing of the helicopter to offer a quantum leap in the tactical mobility and combat power of ground forces. Although the U.S. Army was not the only military institution to exploit the helicopter's vertical lift, range, and speed on the battlefield, it undertook the most comprehensive effort to develop an integrated airmobile force. The main catalyst for this innovation was the desire to provide greater mobility to ground units on both conventional and nuclear battlefields, but airmobility came to have even wider utility.[1]

The first significant tactical use of the helicopter by American forces came during the Korean War. The Marine Corps initially employed light helicopters for observation, casualty evacuation, and similar support missions beginning in August 1950. The Army followed suit later that year. The marines also conducted the inaugural tactical lift of troops in October 1951. The Army deployed two H–19 transport helicopter companies to Korea in the last few months of the conflict, executing its first troop lift in May 1953.[2]

---

[1] The terms *airmobile*, *air assault*, and *air cavalry* have been used variously to describe the same capability, heliborne infantry forces. For simplicity, I have used the term *airmobile*, the one first employed by the Army, throughout the text. John B. Wilson has defined *airmobility* as "the capability of a unit to deploy and receive support from aircraft under the control of a ground commander." See John B. Wilson, *Maneuver and Firepower: The Evolution of Divisions and Separate Brigades*, Army Lineage Series (Washington, D.C.: U.S. Army Center of Military History, 1998), p. 314.

[2] John R. Galvin, *Air Assault: The Development of Airmobile Warfare* (New York: Hawthorne Books, 1969), pp. 261–64; Christopher C. S. Cheng, *Air Mobility: The Development of a Doctrine* (Westport, Conn.: Praeger, 1994), pp. 32–46; Gary W. Parker, *A History of Marine Medium Helicopter Squadron 161* (Washington, D.C.: History and Museums Division, Headquarters, U.S. Marine Corps, 1978), pp. 4–12.

While the Korean War validated the helicopter's role on the conventional battlefield, subsequent Department of Defense and Department of the Army studies sought to explore how best to harness this new technology to tactical nuclear warfare. Army leaders soon reached the conclusion that ground units would have to be highly dispersed to survive a nuclear attack while simultaneously retaining the ability to mass quickly to exploit an atomic strike on opposing forces. Helicopters would provide the mobility that friendly ground troops needed to capitalize on the ensuing shock and disruption of the enemy, without relying on roads and bridges that probably would be damaged in the exchange.[3]

The reorganization of tactical forces became a common theme in various efforts to adapt to the nuclear battlefield. Following the short-lived pentomic division of the late 1950s, the Army began switching to a new organization in 1961. The latter process sought to incorporate reconnaissance aircraft and transport helicopters into all the combat divisions. At the same time, Army leaders had begun a push for specialized airmobile units. In early 1960 the Army Aircraft Requirements Review Board, headed by Lt. Gen. Gordon B. Rogers and thus known as the Rogers Board, evaluated all Army aviation plans for the next decade and solicited ideas from industry. Among its recommendations, the board called for a formal study on the feasibility of what it labeled "air fighting units."[4]

One member of the Rogers Board, Maj. Gen. Hamilton H. Howze, had been a driving force for Army aviation programs for half a decade. Commissioned in the cavalry in 1930, Howze had joined the 1st Armored Division in 1942 and fought with it in North Africa and Italy through the end of the war in Europe. As a brigadier general, he had earned his wings in a special flight course for senior officers and then had become the first director of Army aviation on the Army Staff, serving from February 1955 through December 1957. His office was responsible for preparing budget requests for the development and procurement of Army aircraft. That experience and his background in armored warfare

---

[3] James M. Gavin, *War and Peace in the Space Age* (New York: Harper, 1958), pp. 132–37, 157–60, 193–96; Chang, *Air Mobility*, pp. 59–60.

[4] Wilson, *Maneuver and Firepower*, pp. 263–90; Chang, *Air Mobility*, pp. 61–64; John J. Tolson, *Airmobility, 1961–1971*, Vietnam Studies (Washington, D.C.: Department of the Army, 1973), pp. 8, 9 (quoted words), 10, 16–24.

Maj. Gen. Hamilton H. Howze inspects a helicopter prototype. With the help of Col. Robert R. Williams, Howze focused Army thinking on the role of the helicopter in warfare. *(National Archives)*

made him an early advocate of using both fixed-wing aircraft and helicopters to enhance tactical mobility of ground units.[5]

---

[5] Hamilton H. Howze, *A Cavalryman's Story: Memoirs of a Twentieth-Century Army General* (Washington, D.C.: Smithsonian Institution Press, 1996), pp. 179–95.

In 1957 Howze had prepared a briefing, making a case for what he termed *air cavalry* units. The presentation revolved around a tactical scenario, set in Bavaria, between a reinforced air cavalry brigade and an attacking Soviet armored force. Because the American unit needed neither bridges nor roads, friendly engineers and artillery demolished these avenues of approach. Rather than conduct a conventional linear defense, the brigade used observation aircraft to identify targets for Air Force tactical aircraft, employ transport helicopters to land artillery observers behind enemy lines, attack armored columns with helicopter-launched antitank missiles, and engage the foe in depth with helicopter-borne infantry tank-killer teams.[6]

The Rogers Board paved the way for a more comprehensive study and built momentum for airmobile ground forces, but it would have a direct impact on policy via a more subtle route. The board's secretary, Col. Robert R. Williams, had been on loan from the Army's Office of the Chief of Research and Development, where he headed the Airmobility Division. Commissioned in the field artillery in 1940, he was one of the first officers involved in the fielding of liaison aircraft for air observation, and he ran the flight training program for these pilots at Fort Sill, Oklahoma, from 1942 through July 1944. After the war, he preceded Howze as the Army Staff's aviation proponent in the early 1950s. Following the Rogers Board, Williams served a year in the Office of the Director of Defense Research and Engineering, where he continued to promote Army aviation programs in the Office of the Secretary of Defense.[7]

Williams' efforts found a receptive ear. Secretary of Defense Robert S. McNamara had an interest in ground mobility issues in general and Army aviation in particular. According to Howze, Williams' advocacy resulted in McNamara directing the secretary of the Army on 19 April 1962 to take a comprehensive look at how the Army employed aviation in ground warfare. McNamara's memorandum characterized the Army's aviation programs as too conservative and directed a bold reassessment of aircraft programs, how they integrated with other tactical mobility systems, and what kind of doctrinal innovation was essential to move beyond existing operational and tactical approaches. All existing and projected Army programs were subject to review, with the

---

[6] Howze, *Cavalryman's Story*, pp. 233–36; Cheng, *Air Mobility*, pp. 93–94.
[7] Tolson, *Airmobility*, p. 8.

assumption that the Defense Department would expand Army aviation, if justified. After further prodding from the secretary of defense, the Army's leadership appointed now Lt. Gen. Howze to head the U.S. Army Tactical Mobility Requirements Board (known as the Howze Board). Army aviation advocates, working through a sympathetic secretary of defense, had achieved their goal of forcing the Army's senior leadership to place airmobility on the fast track.[8]

Starting work in late April at Fort Bragg, North Carolina, the Howze Board had until 1 September 1962 to conduct a program of studies, field exercises, experiments, simulations, and operations research, and report back to the secretary of defense. The Continental Army Command extended support to the Howze Board from not only the 82d Airborne Division at Fort Bragg but also other aviation and ground units, including those readying for deployment overseas. Over three intense months the board examined a wide range of organizational and operational concepts for use in both conventional and unconventional warfare, including armed helicopters. Among the conclusions in its report to the secretary of defense, the Howze Board recommended establishment of an airmobile division with 459 aircraft capable of transporting a complete infantry brigade in one lift. Because of the emphasis on helicopters, the division's ground vehicle inventory would decline from 3,452 to 1,100. Other recommendations included establishment of an air cavalry combat brigade with 316 aircraft (including 144 attack helicopters) that would both attack enemy forces and perform traditional cavalry missions of screening and delaying. The Howze Board's ultimate recommendation—that the Army adopt airmobility as a tactical doctrine and organizational principle—was simple and unequivocal, albeit not without controversy.[9]

The Air Force objected immediately. The National Security Act of 1947 and the Defense Reorganization Act of 1958 had left aircraft roles and missions of the two services ill defined. Accelerating technological innovation and changes in organization and doctrine further clouded the situation. During the Korean War, both the Army and Air Force had fielded helicopter units for transporting ground forces. The Army had gained control of the helicopter

---

[8] Ibid., pp. 16–20; Wilson, *Maneuver and Firepower*, pp. 314–18; Howze, *Cavalryman's Story*, pp. 236–37; Cheng, *Air Mobility*, pp. 177–79.

[9] Howze, *Cavalryman's Story*, pp. 238–57; Tolson, *Airmobility*, pp. 20–24.

transport mission by 1956 in exchange for a limitation on the size of Army fixed-wing observation and airlift aircraft. At least two Howze Board recommendations threatened to unravel that agreement—arming the OV–1 Mohawk to conduct what appeared to be close air support missions and procuring the C–7 Caribou fixed-wing transport aircraft. The Air Force questioned many Howze Board proposals and suggested instead a closer joint Army/Air Force effort improve support of conventional infantry divisions with tactical jet aircraft and fixed-wing airlift. McNamara directed a series of joint experiments to explore these options.[10]

Even as the Air Force lodged objections, the Army went ahead with plans to field the first of a recommended five airmobile divisions. McNamara approved the establishment of the new organization on 7 January 1963. The Army quickly activated two test units, the 11th Air Assault Division and the 10th Air Transport Brigade, at Fort Benning, Georgia. Their mission was to refine the Howze Board recommendations regarding the table of organization and equipment required for an airmobile division. During the next two years the Continental Army Command oversaw this effort and also tested aircraft, other materiel, and weapons, using resources from both the understrength 11th Air Assault Division and the 2d Infantry Division, also stationed at Fort Benning.

While the changing operational and tactical environment drove the Army to seek airmobile units, rapidly developing technology spurred force developments. By the early 1960s manufacturers were offering a new generation of helicopters powered by turbine engines that offered major improvements in lift, range, reliability, and ease of maintenance. The Army's hopes rested with the UH–1 Iroquois (known as the Huey), a small transport helicopter designed to carry a squad into battle. The Huey became the workhorse of airmobile units. Equally important, modified Hueys were the first helicopter gunships, filling that role while the Army developed what would become the AH–1 Cobra, a platform dedicated to escorting transport helicopters and providing fire support. Although the Huey gunship proved underpowered for some of its tasks, it demonstrated the range of missions that the gunship could undertake in support of ground units.

---

[10] Cheng, *Air Mobility*, pp. 41–43, 75–77, 106–11, 179–86; Howze, *Cavalryman's Story*, pp. 238–39, 241, 245–47, 254–57; Galvin, *Air Assault*, pp. 278–79; Wilson, *Maneuver and Firepower*, p. 316; Tolson, *Airmobility*, pp. 57–61.

Troops deploy after Sikorsky H–34 helicopters lift off from a landing zone. These early tests at Fort Benning validated the airmobile concept. *(U.S. Army Center of Military History)*

The wide-ranging tests at Fort Benning convinced all but the most obdurate critics that airmobile units had a place in the Army. This type of force had grown indirectly out of the pentomic division's concept of dispersed and nonlinear operations, but proponents saw it as having a wider range of capabilities and strengths. Unlike airborne units, which could attack a deep objective only to have to remain in place awaiting reinforcement and relief by ground forces, the airmobile division could move infantry and artillery as needed. Airmobile formations could mass against an objective from multiple staging areas without providing the same clustered target on a nuclear battlefield as forces operating along conventional lines and without giving an obvious warning to an alert enemy that an attack was forthcoming against a certain sector. They also could jump over heavily defended zones to strike at the enemy's weakest and most vulnerable points. The division's aerial element could more quickly locate enemy units and facilitate engaging them with infantry, armed helicopters, and artillery, all without extensive external coordination. In a similar vein, integrated infantry and helicopter units would develop standard operating procedures for assaults and establish familiarity with each other, thus minimizing coordination problems and permitting rapid responses to fluid tactical situations. Although initially envisioned as operating on conventional and nuclear battlefields in high-intensity theaters of operation, airmobile units offered the promise of being a valuable capability in the unconventional war in Vietnam.[11]

While the Marine Corps had led the way in employing helicopters, it remained focused at this time primarily on vertical lift as a means to transport forces more rapidly to a place where they would fight on the ground. The airmobile concept went a step beyond this approach, developing an integrated air-ground unit that would do as much of its fighting from the sky as it did on land. For instance, the new division had an air cavalry squadron dedicated to reconnaissance, as well as helicopter gunships armed with 2.75-inch rockets—dubbed aerial artillery—to provide fire support for ground troops. Moreover, the capability was entirely organic to the air cavalry division, whereas a Marine division had to obtain aerial assistance from a supporting Marine aircraft wing. The Army's new organization and tactical doctrine, not simply the adoption of the helicopter, made airmobility a true innovation.

In June 1965, despite tests of Air Force support to ground units, the Army persuaded Secretary McNamara to approve the first permanent airmobile division. The Army then cannibalized the skeleton 11th Air Assault Division, 2d Infantry Division, and the 10th Air Transport Brigade to establish the 1st Cavalry Division (Airmobile) on 1 July. The division differed in significant aspects from the Howze Board recommendations, having eight infantry battalions (three airborne qualified), an aerial artillery battalion (in lieu of a general-support field artillery battalion), 425 helicopters, and 6 OV–1 Mohawks (for observation and surveillance missions only). Cobbled together with little time for higher-unit collective training, the 1st Cavalry Division concentrated on attaining full manning and equipment prior to commencing deployment to Vietnam in August.[12]

The test of airmobile units in combat came quickly. The 1st Cavalry Division arrived in September 1965 and was ready for

[11] Galvin, *Air Assault*, pp. 277–78, 286; Tolson, *Airmobility*, pp. 55–57.

[12] Galvin, *Air Assault*, pp. 280–88; Wilson, *Maneuver and Firepower*, pp. 316–18; Tolson, *Airmobility*, pp. 51–57, 59–62; Cheng, *Air Mobility*, pp. 187–88.

operations by the end of the month. It underwent its baptism of fire in late October and November in the Ia Drang Valley, where all three maneuver brigades engaged and repulsed elements of three North Vietnamese Army regiments. The month-long battle began when enemy units encircled the Plei Me Special Forces camp on 19 October, attempting to lure a South Vietnamese relief column from the town of Pleiku, twenty-five miles away. This was the first phase in a Communist attempt to capture the Central Highlands. With extensive U.S. air and artillery support, the South Vietnamese were able to hold Plei Me and defeat the ambush, forcing the North Vietnamese to break the siege on 25 October.

At this point the 1st Cavalry Division joined the search for the withdrawing enemy in the rough country between the camp and the Cambodian border to the west. The division's aerial reconnaissance element, the 1st Squadron, 9th Cavalry, drew first blood on 1 November, capturing a field hospital. Operations continued during the next two weeks with the air cavalry units trying to locate and fix elusive enemy forces that were preparing to resume their attack on Plei Me. The climactic action began on 14 November, when men of the 1st Battalion, 7th Cavalry, assaulted into Landing Zone X-ray, unaware that the North Vietnamese were nearby. Over the next two days, supported by artillery, fixed-wing aircraft, and helicopter gunships, the battalion was able to hold its ground against repeated North Vietnamese assaults. Helicopter transports continued to fly into the beleaguered landing zone, completing the battalion's insertion, making supply runs, and reinforcing the effort with an additional rifle company on the afternoon of the first day. The operation continued through 26 November. During the series of engagements that finally led to the North Vietnamese fleeing into Cambodia, the helicopter proved vital in pursuing the enemy, massing infantry forces to engage him, providing responsive firepower, and supplying units in contact.[13]

---

[13] Tolson, *Airmobility*, pp. 73–83; George C. Herring, "The 1st Cavalry and the Ia Drang Valley, 18 October–24 November 1965," in *America's First Battles, 1776–1965*, ed. Charles E. Heller and William A. Stofft (Lawrence: University Press of Kansas, 1986), pp. 313–19, 325–26; Harold G. Moore and Joseph L. Galloway, *We Were Soldiers Once . . . and Young: Ia Drang—The Battle That Changed the War in Vietnam* (New York: HarperCollins, 1993), pp. 49–236; John M. Carland, *Combat Operations: Stemming the Tide, May 1965 to October 1966*, United States Army in Vietnam (Washington, D.C.: U.S. Army Center of Military History, 2000), pp. 113–34, 361–62.

The division remained in high demand over the next six years in South Vietnam, operating in three of the four military regions before its withdrawal in 1971. Conversion of the 101st Airborne Division to an airmobile configuration during its time in Vietnam was further testament to the value of the concept. Although the Army never followed through on its original goal of fielding five such divisions, it expanded organic helicopter battalions in conventional infantry divisions and established the 1st Aviation Brigade, which provided general support aviation to Army, other-service, and allied units throughout South Vietnam. The airmobile concept had filtered into all Army units in Vietnam.[14]

The establishment of the Army's first airmobile division in 1965 was a significant milestone in enhancing the mobility and combat capability of U.S. ground forces. The close integration of infantry, artillery, transport helicopters, observation aircraft, and gunships within one command yielded a superb degree of tactical flexibility, allowing units to locate the enemy and engage him simultaneously with air and ground combat power. But the value of this innovation had not been obvious to all. While a small group of senior Army aviators had the foresight to see the possibilities and develop the concept, the Army's top-level leadership moved slowly to adopt parts of it and the Air Force opposed it. Stymied by institutional inertia, the visionaries successfully sought aid outside the service to drive implementation at a critical time. The tension between innovators and a chain of command averse to change is a recurring challenge that often requires as much creativity and initiative to solve as did the development of the original concept.

---

[14] Galvin, *Air Assault*, pp. 289–97; Tolson, *Airmobility*, pp. 195–98, 201–04.

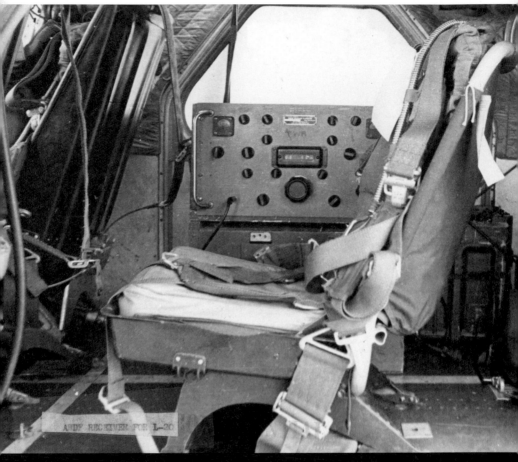

The operator's station in a U–6 Beaver utility plane modified to conduct airborne radio direction finding. Real-time information on the location of enemy units provided a tactical edge to U.S. forces in Vietnam. *(U.S. Army Intelligence and Security Command)*

12

AIRBORNE RADIO DIRECTION FINDING

James L. Gilbert

On 9 May 1961 President John F. Kennedy approved the deployment of the U.S. Army's first unit—the 3d Radio Research Unit (RRU)—to South Vietnam. Its unusual designation was a cover to disguise the presence of an element of the U.S. Army Security Agency (ASA), which had the mission of collecting signals intelligence so U.S. advisers assisting the South Vietnamese Army could help locate an elusive enemy in the jungle and mountains that covered much of the country. Because the South Vietnamese had reported great success in their own signals intelligence efforts, the Army Security Agency anticipated no problems. However, the Americans soon discovered that their allies had exaggerated their claims and that it would take major effort and a new type of intelligence collection asset to provide useful information.[1]

The difficult signals environment in Vietnam would dictate how the Army Security Agency eventually fought the war in the ether. Because much of the terrain was hilly or mountainous or covered by dense, tall foliage, the Communist guerrillas, or Viet Cong, could not normally use radio frequencies that depended upon a favorable line of sight. Direct or ground waves would only travel five to fifteen miles at most. The enemy at lower echelons (regiment and battalion) also generally had to rely on the simple resources at his disposal—often small homemade transmitters powered by hand-cranked or pedaled generators. Under these circumstances, the best way to communicate was to employ signals in the high frequency range using antennas made from horizontal wires. This system projected skywave signals up to the ionosphere where an electrically charged layer bounced them back

---

[1] This chapter is based on James L. Gilbert, *The Most Secret War: Army Signals Intelligence in Vietnam* (Fort Belvoir, Va.: U.S. Army Intelligence and Security Command, 2003). While the book is unclassified, many of the primary sources underlying it have not yet been declassified.

down to receiving stations, bypassing the obstacles of vegetation and terrain.

Using well-honed normally reliable methods, the 3d RRU planned to pinpoint the origin of these high frequency signals and thus the location of enemy units. The American outfit established a handful of semipermanent direction-finding sites throughout South Vietnam and then linked them together to form a net. Upon being alerted that a certain enemy station was broadcasting, the sites took a bearing on the signal to determine the direction from which it was emanating. They could not ascertain how far away the enemy station was but could plot the bearings from their respective locations, theoretically generating a point where three or more lines crossed—known as a fix.

In this case the direction-finding net simply did not work. Because the ionosphere is not a perfectly smooth reflecting surface, signals bounced from a transmitter closer than a few hundred miles from a direction-finding station often appear to come from an entirely wrong direction. In addition, the direction-finding systems produced large errors when receiving anything other than vertically polarized signals; the enemy skywaves were mostly horizontally polarized. At best, instead of intersecting at a point, the bearings outlined an area, supplying fixes with diameters ranging upward from five miles to more than thirty. Often the results were completely useless. Launching any combat operation without more precise coordinates would waste valuable resources, for the troops would have to scour many square miles.

The 3d RRU first tried to solve this difficulty by slightly altering tactics. Having acquired a general location from the net of direction-finding stations, mobile teams went out to obtain more accurate fixes. When the enemy station transmitted again (often on the same frequency and same schedule), hopefully the mobile elements would be near enough to pick up ground waves that would allow them to pinpoint the location. However, because the Viet Cong were using antennas that projected most of the signal upwards, the direction finders had to be very close to receive sufficient ground wave signal. That same proximity to the enemy made the teams vulnerable to attack, and it did not take long before the Viet Cong targeted them. In December 1961 guerrillas ambushed a combined South Vietnamese/American direction-finding team, killing ten members. The final blow to the original concept of operations was the response of the South Vietnamese Army. Given the failure of their own direction-finding efforts, the South

Vietnamese were reluctant to commit troops based on such intelligence, and they did not have the transportation assets to react in a timely manner even when they decided to do something.

The Army Security Agency had to find a new method of quickly and accurately locating the enemy in this challenging environment. Up to this point, most research and development had been focused on detecting Soviet very high frequency transmissions in Europe and was not applicable to the situation in South Vietnam. The headquarters staff at Arlington Hall Station, Virginia, studied several possible solutions, including upgrading current direction-finding systems, creating a new semipermanent net spread out over a wider area, and developing a backpack model for use in the field. The staff also considered airborne radio direction finding, but initially thought of it only as a last resort. Technical experience told them that the metal skin of an aircraft would degrade the ability of a high frequency direction finder to perform accurately, having to deal with both direct signals transmitted from the ground and the skywaves bounced back from the ionosphere.

ASA research and development engineer Herbert S. Hovey Jr. teamed up with two counterparts at the U.S. Army Electronics Command, Harold M. Jaffe and John Woodworth, to find a solution. The three men had collaborated in the past on other projects. Hovey had earned an electronics engineering degree from the University of Florida, served two years of active duty in the late 1950s as a lieutenant at the Army Security Agency, and was still in the Army Reserves. A "technical genius," he also had the ability to inspire his subordinates to excel.[2] Jaffe was a self-trained engineer who had never been to college. He had gotten his start in the Army Signal Corps in World War II, rising to the rank of staff sergeant. For his part in establishing a communications system for the Belgian resistance, Belgium awarded him the Croix de Guerre. What he lacked in formal education he made up in intelligence, resourcefulness, and tenacity. He also had a facility for breaking down problems and ideas into clear and simple terms.[3]

---

[2] E-mails, Thomas N. Hauser to Jon Hoffman, 23 May 2007, and Tom Hurt to Jon Hoffman, 30 Mar 2009 (quoted words), Historians files, U.S. Army Center of Military History (CMH), Washington D.C.; *The Florida Engineer*, Fall/Winter 2006, p. 28.

[3] Service Record, Harold M. Jaffe, National Personnel Records Center, St. Louis, Mo. See also Memo, Clyde D. Harkin, Director, Electronics Warfare Lab, for Friends of Harold Jaffe, 16 May 1978, sub: Retirement; Ltr, Michele Janka, Embassy of Belgium, to Jon Hoffman, 18 Oct 2007, sub: Croix de Guerre with Palm—Mr.

At a Saigon airfield Herbert S. Hovey Jr. *(second from left)* and other engineers stand in front of a U–6 equipped with the first operational radio direction-finding set. The vertical dipole antenna is visible on the near wing. *(Harold Jaffe / U.S. Army Intelligence and Security Command)*

The engineers' first priority was to travel to South Vietnam in November 1961 to gain an appreciation of the signals conditions and evaluate alternative methods. They determined that designing and fielding a new type of ground system would take too much time. Establishing a wider net of direction-finding stations would be comparatively easy, but not necessarily better given the problems inherent in dealing with horizontally polarized signals. They concluded that an airborne direction-finding system offered more flexibility and more accuracy.

Once they returned to the United States, the engineers took a first stab at the problem by installing a direction finder in a UH–19 Chickasaw helicopter, but vibration caused them to reject

Harold Jaffe; Ltr, David Noyes to Jon Hoffman, 14 May 2007, sub: Harold Jaffe; and Harold M. Jaffe obituary, undated. All in Historians files, CMH.

the platform. They next tried a U–6A, a small fixed-wing aircraft nicknamed the Beaver and traditionally used for artillery spotting or transporting senior officers; numerous U–6s were in Vietnam, which meant that maintenance support was readily available. The planes could carry an air crew of two, plus a small amount of direction-finding equipment and an operator.

The engineers soon settled upon a simple but ingenious answer to the main shortcoming of an aerial platform—the interference from its metal skin. When they vertically mounted a dipole antenna (a single rod several feet in length) on the leading edge of each of the U–6's wings, they found that the problem with interference largely disappeared. A feed cable from each dipole brought the antenna output into the cabin, where the two were combined in a process that fed the difference between them into an R–390 high frequency receiver. When the two antenna outputs were identical, they canceled each other and the receiver audio fell to zero (called a null). A null occurred whenever the aircraft was flying either directly toward or directly away from the target radio.

When the operator began receiving a signal of interest, he notified the pilot, who was also listening to the receiver audio. The pilot then flew the plane into a flat turn (as the wings had to remain parallel to the ground to obtain a usable bearing) and, upon hearing a null, reversed course into an opposite flat turn to reacquire the null. He kept up the process as the operator listened and read the azimuth from the aircraft's gyrocompass. When the operator was certain he had a bearing to the target radio, he then immediately notified the copilot, whose job it was to determine the location of the aircraft at that moment. The copilot, who had to rely solely upon matching what he saw on the ground below to a map (a difficult process in areas without prominent terrain features to serve as reference points), plotted that point on the map and drew the bearing from it based on the azimuth provided by the operator. The crew then flew to different locations and repeated the process, producing additional bearings on the map until they developed a fix. It took a lot of skill and teamwork to generate good results, not to mention steady stomachs to handle the rapid flat turns that veered quickly from one side to the other.[4]

In March 1962, after testing the concept with great success in the United States, the engineers carried the equipment in their suitcases on a return trip to South Vietnam, where aircraft and

---

[4] E-mail, David Noyes to Jon Hoffman, 16 May 2007, Historians files, CMH.

Harold M. Jaffe accompanies a planeload of radio direction-finding equipment destined to outfit aircraft in Vietnam. The deployment of the civilian engineers to the war zone solved problems that might have killed the program in its infancy. *(Joan Hand/U.S. Army Center of Military History)*

pilots had been assembled. They immediately ran into problems. An initial challenge was simply keeping the antennas on the wings in flight. More surprising, the engineers discovered that the early trials in Vietnam did not yield the same outstanding results. Further investigation revealed that two out of every three U–6s had undergone some structural repair or modification, and these changes to the airframes were hindering their use as direction-finding platforms. In some cases the problem was as basic as differences in the amount of paint on the two wings, which made the current distribution uneven. Switching to U–6s still in their original configuration soon got the development program back on track.[5] The engineers later pondered what might have happened if, during the initial testing in the United States, they had employed an aircraft that had undergone some alteration. Given less than

---

[5] Dennis Buley, "The Beginning of ARDF," copy in Historians files, CMH.

impressive returns, they might have altogether abandoned the airborne radio direction-finding project.

From the initial operational flight in Vietnam in April 1962, the 3d RRU's airborne radio direction-finding efforts provided dramatic results. For the first time, the Army had a signals intelligence system that could find enemy units in a timely fashion and with enough accuracy to guide tactical operations. The commander of the U.S. Military Assistance Command, Vietnam, Lt. Gen. Paul D. Harkins, summed up the contribution being made by the new method: "One of the biggest disadvantages to any counter-insurgency program has been the inability to locate guerrilla concentrations. The direction-finding activities of the 3d Radio Research Unit have provided this headquarters with a vital intelligence advantage previously unavailable to any U.S. or friendly tactical force."[6] Successful combat actions based on airborne signals intelligence resulted in the Army awarding the first Meritorious Unit Commendation of the war to the 3d RRU.

The men who put together this success were not about to rest on their laurels. Because the early systems could be created in-house without significant funding, the airborne program grew as rapidly as engineers could hand-carry the equipment to Vietnam and install it there. As important, they soon adopted the twin-engine U–8 Seminole aircraft as the workhorse of the direction-finding effort. It could operate in a wider range of weather; fly higher and thus provide better coverage in the mountainous regions; and had the additional load capacity to carry navigational gear, which eliminated the need to rely on visual landmarks when plotting bearings.

The year 1965 was a defining one for airborne direction-finding. The Air Force began to deploy platforms, and together the two services contributed over 130 aircraft to the signals intelligence effort. To coordinate the use of airborne intercept and to order missions, the Military Assistance Command established an Airborne Radio Direction Finding Center in Saigon. The introduction of American combat forces with much greater mobility provided a capability to react more rapidly to the intelligence acquired. The year also witnessed the first use of Army aircraft in direct support of a combat operation while it was still in progress. The U.S. Marines were engaging a Viet Cong regiment in Operation STARLITE. Alerted by ASA units on the ground, direction-finding aircraft targeted the

---

[6] Gilbert, *Most Secret War*, p.16.

enemy's transmitters and proceeded to track his movements. The commander of the III Marine Amphibious Force later lauded the "accuracy and timeliness of the intelligence produced."[7]

Over the next seven years, the Army fielded seven different direction-finding systems in a variety of aircraft. A unique approach, consisting of newer electronics equipment installed in a UH–1D Huey helicopter, not only overcame the early problems with vibration but also produced even more accurate fixes than fixed-wing platforms. It was a collaboration between the signals intelligence units, which contributed the operators and electronics systems, and the supported combat divisions, which furnished the aircraft and crew. The Hueys flew in direct support of their respective divisions, thus providing the most responsive asset to ground commanders. As soon as an operator called in a fix, an observation chopper searched the area for evidence of movement, trail use, or bunkers. If the enemy were spotted, troops could be inserted almost immediately.

Throughout the war, the Army airborne radio direction-finding program continued to embrace new technological advances to identify enemy locations. But perhaps the most important steps were taken in the arena of friendly communications. In the beginning, airplanes had to land to pass on intelligence to waiting tactical commanders; the direction-finding crews did not use radios because the enemy might listen in and learn of his vulnerability to direction finding. This slow process for transferring information obviously delayed action. Next, crews used one-time pads to pass encrypted messages back and forth to ground units by radio. This simple system, consisting of different code keys printed on each page, prevented the enemy from understanding what was being transmitted. Once used, the page would be destroyed. However, it was a slow and cumbersome method for passing along significant amounts of information. In 1967 the Army Security Agency installed voice encryption equipment in the planes; it then took just six minutes from the moment a fix was determined until it was in the hands of a tactical commander.

At the height of the war, Army airborne radio direction-finding platforms were contributing some four thousand fixes a month. Many of these could not be tied to an identifiable unit, but they could still be used in pattern analysis where accumulation of dots on a map over time suggested activity and movement. Based on

---

[7] Ibid., p. 35.

analysis of this type of information, U.S. troops went on partial alert on the eve of the 1968 Tet Offensive.

Surveys of U.S. commanders indicated that signals intelligence (which included not only airborne radio direction finding but also other methods as well) accounted for as much as 90 percent of the timely usable intelligence. Captured documents and interrogated prisoners were also important sources, but often by-products of a successful direction-finding mission. Airborne radio direction finding was not foolproof; the enemy employed a number of methods to minimize the risk of being pinpointed or to throw off the hunters with false leads. As in most cases of innovation, it was a process marked by ongoing interplay between the two sides as each reacted and adapted to the other. Even so, the new capability created by Hovey, Jaffe, and Woodworth proved to be a valuable asset throughout the war. Army Vice Chief of Staff General Bruce Palmer Jr. summed up the impact of these programs: "Field commanders in Vietnam continue to say that this is the backbone of their intelligence effort. They can't live or fight without it. I want to stress to everyone in this room just how important this effort is. . . . I can't think of anything more important because they are just blind over there without this effort."[8]

---

[8] Memo, Gen Bruce Palmer Jr. for Maj D.L. Parsons, undated [1975], sub: Army Airborne Radio Direction Finding During Vietnam War, Historical Research Collection, U.S. Army Intelligence and Security Command, Fort Belvoir, Va.

M114 155-mm. howitzers deployed at Firebase MEGAN in Vietnam in 1969. The requirement to fire on short notice in all directions posed a challenge for the big guns. *(National Archives)*

13

ARTILLERY SPEED SHIFTER

Terry L. Beckenbaugh

One of the tactical mainstays of the Vietnam war was the firebase. Sometimes permanent and sometimes carved out of jungle, rice paddies, or rough terrain in a matter of hours just for a particular operation, these relatively small outposts were dedicated to providing artillery support to infantry units anywhere within range. And therein lay the challenge, for in the absence of the front lines common in a more typical conflict, the tubes in this unconventional war had to be able to fire in any direction at a moment's notice. The standard 105-mm. howitzer was reasonably well suited to this role, but its heavier towed 155-mm. cousin was not. If a mission were outside the latter's existing fan of fire (limited to 800 mils or 45 degrees), the crew had to lower the piece from its firing jack, lift the trails, swing it into the new position, and get it set again to fire. Even with a full complement of eight soldiers and optimal conditions, this cumbersome procedure could take several minutes—precious time when American and allied infantrymen were engaged with the enemy. But a complete crew was seldom on hand, and more often rain and mud created an unstable ground surface that made the howitzer extremely difficult to move.

A solution would come from 1st Lt. Nathaniel W. Foster Jr., a champion cross-country runner and Reserve Officer Training Corps graduate of Central State University in Wilberforce, Ohio.[1] In 1966 Foster was serving in Vietnam as the executive officer of Battery B, 8th Battalion, 6th Artillery—a 155-mm. towed outfit of the 1st Infantry Division—and was certain there had to be a quicker more efficient way to shift the howitzer to respond to the fast-moving requirements of combat. He was aware that U.S.

---

[1] Telecon, Mark J. Reardon with Keith A. Perkins, Central State University, 29 Jul 2009, Historians files, U.S. Army Center of Military History (CMH), Washington, D.C.

Army Weapons Command was looking at some form of pedestal to bear the weight of the piece so it could spin more easily and rapidly, but he took it upon himself to find an immediate answer in the field rather than waiting for the bureaucracy at home to develop the perfect solution. He attacked the problem methodically, determining that the first order of business was to find the point of balance of the howitzer. He and his soldiers started with the tube of the test weapon at an elevation of 300 mils, the standard setting when initially aiming it. They simply kept moving the firing jack until their experiments revealed that the point of balance of the howitzer was two feet seven inches to the rear of the standard location for the jack.

With that knowledge in hand, the officers and men of the battery began work on a prototype speed-shifting device. Because they did not have the proper tools, they had to take a howitzer during downtime to a maintenance shop, where Pfc. Charles Harkness of the battery's fire direction center did the welding.[2] The initial attempt was very simple, a metal collar fixed under the howitzer at its point of balance and a pedestal consisting of a torsion bar welded to the base of a firing jack. When the soldiers lowered the piece from the regular firing jack onto the tip of the torsion bar, they found that they could shift the howitzer with a minimum of physical effort using handspikes in the appropriate sockets of the trails. Two could move the 155-mm. through an entire 360-degree circle in just nineteen seconds. Even adding in the time to raise and lower the firing jack before and after the shift, the job could be completed faster than other tasks required to execute a firing mission, such as computation of the firing data.

The inventors had first considered the possibility of simply placing the firing jack at the point of balance, but soon realized that option provided an unstable platform. The firing jack needed to be in its designed spot to force the weight of the piece back on the trails during firing, thus solidly anchoring it for recoil. During shifting the howitzer maintained a tenuous balance on the torsion bar and could easily tip, but the wheels and the partly retracted firing jack prevented it from going too far in any direction. The battery also considered mounting the entire speed shifter, instead of just the collar, to the underside of the carriage, but reasoned

---

[2] E-mails, Frank P. Long Jr. to Terry Beckenbaugh and Jon Hoffman, Aug–Sep 2005, Historians files, CMH.

An artilleryman raises the firing jack *(front)* to lower the gun onto the speed jack *(rear)*. The latter device was simple, and artillery batteries fabricated them in Vietnam as the concept spread throughout the war zone. *(National Archives)*

that such a projection would be a hindrance in any off-road setting with rough terrain or dense undergrowth.

Not satisfied with this initial success, the battery kept testing and evaluating its procedures as well as the device itself. The soldiers discovered that the process worked most smoothly when they unlocked the wheels and raised the firing jack up just enough to let the trail spades rise about a foot off the ground during shifting. This minimized the time spent raising and lowering the firing jack and reduced the likelihood of tipping. Based on experience, Foster also decided that an adjustable pedestal for the speed shifter was necessary. If a previous fire mission had forced the trail spades too deeply into the ground, there sometimes was not enough clearance to get a fixed pedestal back under the carriage.

Foster and his men thus built an entirely new device, using a road wheel from an armored personnel carrier as the base and an 8-ton hydraulic jack in place of the torsion bar. When the upper piston of the extendable two-piece jack proved susceptible to snapping off, they fabricated a single piston of the same over-all length to replace it. Taken together, the procedures and new device reduced the shifting time even further. Still, they found the jack lacked enough weight-bearing capacity, resulting in hydrau-lic fluid leaking from the seals.

The next version used a 25-ton screw-and-ratchet jack. The soldiers built a large base for it and used a lathe to create a rotat-ing surface for the jack head, thus improving the swivel capabil-ity of the howitzer. The strength and nonhydraulic nature of the new jack allowed the battery to leave its howitzers resting on the speed-shifter between fire missions without concern for deteriora-tion of the device. With the firing jack raised a few inches above the ground and handspikes already attached to the trails, even a very short-handed crew could shift a weapon in this condition in a matter of seconds to any direction. Once the howitzer was in the proper position, or if the fire mission required no shift, one soldier simply lowered the shifting jack while another raised the firing jack until it bore the weight of the weapon. The men of Battery B were so confident in the utility of their device that they believed they could shift faster than their smaller 105-mm. brethren and even rival the speed of self-propelled howitzers using powered turrets.

The invention immediately demonstrated its effectiveness in combat. Shortly after Operation BIRMINGHAM ended in May 1966, Foster summarized the success of his battery in action in War Zone C along the Cambodian border:

> One gun by actual count shifted a total of 33 times in 16 hours to fire for advancing infantry of the 1st Division. They [the speed shifters] were used under fire to swing around and bring direct fire upon attacking VC [Viet Cong] in a matter of seconds. This battery, with the use of these jacks and adjustable pedestals, has on this operation expended over 7,200 rounds and shifted day and night for 19 days with an average crew of 6 men including the chief of section. This shifting was done in rice fields that caused the trucks and howitzers to become stuck countless times.

The branch magazine *Artillery Trends* seconded this high praise, noting that the "radically new concept" was verified by

Two soldiers easily maneuver their six-ton howitzer into firing position. The speed jack saved precious seconds in providing fire support to troops in contact. *(National Archives)*

"the most valid test," having "proven its worth . . . under actual combat conditions."[3]

By the summer of 1966 the entire 8th Battalion was using the speed shifter to improve the delivery of fire support. As word of its usefulness spread, the device (or locally fabricated variants of it) came into common use in 155-mm. units throughout Vietnam. While its impact on the overall course of the war was not measurable, the speed shifter enhanced the effectiveness of the firebase concept. After the war Lt. Gen. John H. Hay Jr., who had commanded the 1st Infantry Division in Vietnam, lauded the 155-mm. speed shifter as a prime "example of the ingenuity of artillery innovations."[4]

---

[3] Nathaniel W. Foster, "Speed Shifting the 155-mm. Howitzer, Towed: The Evolution of an Idea," *Artillery Trends,* January 1967, p. 17.

[4] John H. Hay Jr., *Tactical and Materiel Innovations*, Vietnam Studies (Washington, D.C.: Department of the Army, 1974), pp. iv, 53 (quoted words).

Changes in procedures also enhanced the responsiveness of the howitzers. The organization responsible for doctrine promulgated one such adaptation. The Gunnery Department of the Army Artillery and Missile School at Fort Sill, Oklahoma, established a standard method for fire direction centers to plot targets and develop firing solutions in all directions. Units in the field came up with other innovations on their own. A common one among light and medium batteries was to lay their six guns in pairs spaced about 2100 mils (or 120 degrees) apart. When a mission came in, the two pieces pointed closest to the required direction would fire the adjusting rounds. By the time they were on target, the rest of the battery would have used the speed shifters to reposition and be ready to fire for effect.[5]

I Field Force Artillery commander Brig. Gen. Willis D. Crittenberger Jr. aptly described Vietnam as "largely a battery commander's war." Crittenberger believed that "the junior officer must really be on his toes, thinking ahead," because support from higher echelons was always a long way off. He felt certain that this conflict thus served as "a great training ground for the leaders of the future."[6] In 1966 Foster was definitely "on his toes" and not waiting for direction from above or support from the rear. He and his men recognized a need and manufactured their own solution, thus saving the lives of countless fellow soldiers and undoubtedly affecting the outcome of numerous engagements. The inventors of the speed shifter amply demonstrated the capability of junior leaders and soldiers to identify problems or shortcomings, to come up with their own solutions, and to make a positive impact far beyond their own unit.

---

[5] E-mail, John Moltz to Jon Hoffman, 24 Jul 2007, Historians files, CMH.
[6] Hay, *Innovations*, pp. 53–54; David Ewing Ott, *Field Artillery, 1954–1973*, Vietnam Studies (Washington, D.C.: Department of the Army, 1975), p. 70.

An M2 Bradley infantry fighting vehicle leads a column of M1 Abrams tanks across the desert at the National Training Center, Fort Irwin, California. After Vietnam the Army not only acquired much better equipment but also revolutionized training. *(National Training Center)*

14
NATIONAL TRAINING CENTER

Anne W. Chapman

Throughout much of the U.S. Army's history it had entered wars in a state of unreadiness, often for reasons beyond its control. One recurring factor was the need to vastly expand a small peacetime force, using part-time soldiers and raw recruits. This requirement drove the design of the Army's training system throughout much of the twentieth century, but the challenge of combat nearly always exceeded the level of preparation. Following the end of the Vietnam war a few senior leaders in the Army, particularly General William E. DePuy and Maj. Gen. Paul F. Gorman, vowed to revolutionize doctrine and training to enhance preparation for the next conflict. The capstone achievement of their effort was establishment of the National Training Center at Fort Irwin, California, in 1980.[1]

A number of factors spurred DePuy and Gorman to action. They believed the Army would have to fight outnumbered against its next likely opponent, the Warsaw Pact, so each U.S. soldier would have to be better than his adversary. They were certain that the Israeli victory in the 1973 Yom Kippur War validated the importance of individual and small-unit skill in a battle against a more numerous enemy. The generals knew that the existing Army Training Program, which required that subjects be taught for a set number of hours in a building-block approach starting at the individual level, was outmoded. Future conflict would not provide a long period for mobilization and unit training prior to combat, while wartime individual rotation policies required soldiers to be ready to fight as part of a team when they joined their outfits. DePuy, commander of the newly established U.S. Army Training and Doctrine Command, also was pushing development of new

---

[1] This chapter is drawn from Anne W. Chapman, *The Origins and Development of the National Training Center, 1976–1984* (Fort Monroe, Va.: U.S. Army Training and Doctrine Command, 1992).

doctrine (published in 1976 as Field Manual 100–5, *Operations*) that emphasized the importance of combined arms operations in the increasingly lethal and more fluid environment of modern war. Performing more complex duties in more challenging situations dictated that soldiers be much better prepared than their predecessors. Gorman, DePuy's deputy chief of staff for training, addressed one aspect of this training requirement with creation of the Army Training and Evaluation Program. A performance-oriented system, it required soldiers and units to execute tasks to an acceptable standard, not just undergo a fixed amount of instruction.

New doctrine and a new training system were only part of the solution, however. The evaluation of unit performance required a pool of observers; a means for them to gather and evaluate data; and, ideally, a numerically superior opposing force—imitating enemy tactics and capabilities—to add realism. The increasing range of modern weapons and the resulting dispersion of forces on the battlefield also demanded large spaces for maneuver and live fire. Such resources were simply not available at local Army commands. Establishing the ability to conduct realistic training would not only solve these issues but also provide a means for evaluating and incorporating the many new weapons the Army would begin to acquire in the late 1970s.

The commander of the U.S. Army Forces Command, General Bernard W. Rogers, supplied the seed of a solution. Addressing the space issue, Rogers suggested that the Army not attempt to acquire expensive land around most existing bases but designate a central training facility at a post already large enough to support unfettered fire and maneuver. Units would go there on a rotating basis. Gorman developed and expanded this idea in a November 1976 paper calling for a combined arms training center. The concept borrowed in part from Navy and Air Force programs (the Naval Fighter Weapons School, nicknamed Top Gun, and the Air Force Tactical Fighter Weapons Center's Red Flag exercises) that used instrumented ranges and dedicated opposing forces to improve the skills of air crews. The Army's version would bring elements of a brigade, with a full slice of supporting forces, to a national training center, to conduct a force-on-force exercise against a unit operating with Soviet doctrine and Soviet-type equipment. Experienced observers and modern simulation technology would add realism and ensure superior feedback. While a few other nations had large centralized ground-training facilities, none would approach the sophistication and quality of the Army's proposed training center.

The concept won quick approval from the Army vice chief of staff on 11 April 1977. The desired site was Fort Irwin, an installation of a thousand square miles in the high desert of California that was bigger than the state of Rhode Island. Its location near Nellis Air Force Base (home of the Red Flag exercises) would facilitate the integration of fixed-wing air support into the Army program. Training and Doctrine Command and Army Forces Command shared responsibility for developing and implementing a plan to create the training center. The Defense Advanced Research Projects Agency, the Air Force Tactical Air Command, and the Army's Materiel Development and Readiness Command (later, Army Materiel Command) contributed to the effort.

As with most innovative ideas, the concept had to clear a number of hurdles before it became reality. Organizationally, the division of responsibility between two major commands brought about disagreements and disjointed action. It took the establishment in May 1980 of a general officer steering committee, jointly chaired by the deputy commanders of the two organizations, to make the process work effectively. California officials initially opposed the site for environmental reasons, while an attempt to annex 300,000 adjacent acres of the Mojave Desert ran afoul of private groups concerned about an endangered tortoise. Some members of Congress feared the program might result in the loss of bases and jobs in their districts. Cost overruns only added to this difficult political atmosphere. While Fort Irwin was ideal as a training area, it had been in a caretaker status for many years and lacked any modern infrastructure to support permanent personnel. The price of making the base habitable thus ballooned far beyond initial estimates. Reliance on relatively new technology for instrumentation of ranges also resulted in unforeseen cost increases and delays. Air Force participation proved difficult to arrange due to problems of incorporating aircraft into the instrumentation system and disagreements about the provision of close air support. Creating a new base and command also put stress on the manpower system.

On the positive side, the program proved visionary. In 1979 events in Afghanistan and Iran focused the United States on the task of renewing its military power for potential combat against the Soviets or Middle Eastern states. Additional money and manpower became available for Fort Irwin as resources flowed into national defense in the early 1980s, just in time to establish a premier training program when the Army and the nation felt it was most needed.

The first U.S. Army maneuver battalions conducted exercises at the National Training Center in the latter half of 1981. Initially each training cycle, known as a rotation, featured two heavy battalion task forces (one armor and one mechanized infantry) supported by field artillery, attack helicopters, and Air Force planes. The parent brigade headquarters participated by controlling the battalions in a command post exercise. Over time rotations began to feature light infantry, cavalry, and motorized units.

To accomplish the mission of training soldiers in a setting as close as possible to the reality of combat, the National Training Center based its program on three pillars—a dedicated opposing force, a group of experienced officers and soldiers serving as exercise observer/controllers, and a sophisticated instrumentation system to gather data and provide the raw material for assessing unit performance.

The opposing force consisted of two Army heavy battalions (one infantry and one armor) permanently stationed at Fort Irwin. They were originally configured for battle as the Soviet *32d Guards Motorized Rifle Regiment* and considerably outnumbered the rotating outfit, known as the Blue Force. For the most part, the vehicles were U.S. equipment visually modified to resemble Soviet tanks, personnel carriers, air defense systems, light reconnaissance vehicles, and helicopters. The outfit modeled its battle doctrine and tactics on the Warsaw Pact forces (until some later scenarios reflected lessons learned in Operation DESERT STORM). The pseudo-enemy soldiers were no straw men that would roll over and play dead; in fact, they almost always defeated the Blue Force. While part of that outcome was simply the home-field advantage from knowing the terrain and the scenario, one center commander pointed out the value of having a strong opposing force:

> He must be good enough so that BLUEFOR can't make major mistakes and win. Otherwise, you can't take the lessons from NTC and apply them with any confidence in war. If you win because the OPFOR can't cross the line of departure, if you win because the OPFOR can't use artillery, if you win because the OPFOR maneuvers poorly or loses command and control, you don't know whether your victory is meaningful. In war we would be happy to take victories like that.[2]

---

[2] Interv, Capt Ferdinand Irizarry, Opns Off, Observation Div, National Training Center (NTC), with Brig Gen Wesley K. Clark, Cdr, NTC, Sep 1992, History Office, U.S. Army Training and Doctrine Command (TRADOC), Fort Monroe, Va.

A Sheridan tank rigged to look like a BMP armored vehicle moves into position at the National Training Center. A well-prepared opposing force, equipped with visually modified weaponry to simulate a Soviet unit, added realism to the training. *(National Training Center)*

The observer/controllers were U.S. Army officers and noncommissioned officers on regular assignment to the National Training Center. A team accompanied each battalion task force throughout its rotation at Fort Irwin. The observer/controllers refereed the free-play battles, assessed results, and conducted an after action review at the conclusion of each engagement. Other personnel acted as training analysts in the central operations center.

To achieve realism and collect data from engagements, the National Training Center relied upon a complex system of computers, laser-engagement devices, and communications networks. The Multiple Integrated Laser Engagement System simulated fire,

registered hits and near misses, and provided a degree of realism
in casualty assessment eclipsed only by actual combat. The communications network automatically gathered laser-engagement
data and other information, feeding it directly into computer ter-
minals at the operations center. Analysts there could observe the
battle and communicate with controllers in the field as the action
unfolded. The observer/controllers also made good use of the
data in preparing after action reviews. The sophisticated instrumentation system helped both the evaluators and the Blue Force
determine what happened, why it happened, and how to correct
deficiencies before the next battle.

The after action review was probably the single major influence on the revolution in training that took place in the Army in
the twenty years following the Vietnam War. The National Training
Center firmly established it as a formal and valuable method and
helped propagate the review process as an evaluation tool throughout the Army by the mid-1990s. The center's observer/controllers
conducted reviews at platoon, company, and battalion levels, as
well as for supporting elements. The reviews drew on both com-
puter-generated information and subjective field observations to
determine the causes for failure on the simulated battlefield. More
than one battalion commander found the reviews to be "brutally
honest."[3] Reporters characterized the process as "a military group
therapy session" and "a warfare class for the MTV generation."[4]
Another correspondent came closest to capturing the contribution
the after action reviews made to improved training:

> "Sir," the young lieutenant begins, "I don't really think the com-
> mander made clear exactly what his intent was." After a moment's
> uncomfortable silence, Gen Barry McCaffrey, then commander of
> the 24th Infantry Division, speaks up. "That's a good point," he
> acknowledges. "Getting our purpose across is key." Suffice it to say
> that 10 years ago, a young Army officer was just as likely to commit
> hara-kiri as to openly criticize his commanding officer.[5]

The National Training Center also featured one of the Army's
most sophisticated live-fire ranges. Located in the northern portion
of Fort Irwin, the site gave rotating units the opportunity to attack

---

[3] J. R. Wilson, "National Training Center," *Jane's Defence Weekly*, 23 Feb 1991,
p. 261.

[4] Ibid. (first quoted words); Notes (second quoted words), MTV (Music
Television) program, Historians files, History Office, TRADOC.

[5] Wilson, "National Training Center," *Jane's Defence Weekly*, 23 Feb 1991, p. 261.

Observer/controllers at the end of a mission conduct an after action review with members of a tank platoon at the National Training Center. The frank critique of the training reinforced the experience gained. *(National Training Center)*

a position or defend it against a simulated advancing force. Troops could employ the full spectrum of small arms, tank, and artillery fire against approximately 1,500 computerized, radio-controlled, pop-up targets that simulated the appearance, thermal signature, and firepower of a Soviet-style motorized rifle regiment. Some of the targets had the ability to shoot back with simulated tank fire and antitank missiles.

In the summer of 1984 Army Chief of Staff General John A. Wickham declared the innovative training center a success. No single training development since World War II had had so profound an impact on the readiness of the U.S. Army's fighting battalions. By introducing Army units to an unprecedented combat realism under rigorous Spartan field conditions, coupled with a thoroughgoing evaluation system, the center provided a degree of insight into unit performance never previously available. This unique training and evaluation system also stood as a tribute to the systems-based hands-on approach that had dominated Army training since General DePuy's tenure at the Training and Doctrine Command in the mid-1970s.

The success of the National Training Center had a ripple effect. In 1987 the Army established a similar facility for light forces. The Joint Readiness Training Center, originally at Fort Chaffee, Arkansas, and later at Fort Polk, Louisiana, also featured an opposing force. A year later the Army started planning for the Combat Maneuver Training Center at Hohenfels, Germany, to provide troops in Europe the same realistic training exercises as Fort Irwin. Meanwhile, the Army began developing the Battle Command Training Program, a simulation-driven command post exercise to train corps commanders. The four programs soon came under a single umbrella, the Combat Training Centers, which provided the Army with the capability to train heavy, light, and special operations forces across the spectrum of conflict.[6] In 1985, to determine relevant lessons from the performance of units at the National Training Center and to disseminate that knowledge to other commands, the Army launched the Center for Army Lessons Learned at the Combined Arms Center at Fort Leavenworth, Kansas.

The outstanding record of the Army in Operations DESERT STORM and IRAQI FREEDOM was built on experience at the National Training Center and at the other Combat Training Centers it spawned. More recently Fort Irwin has hosted advanced warfighting experiments, served as a test-bed for the Army's new Stryker wheeled vehicle, and provided a realistic preparatory experience for troops deploying to the war in Iraq. The most costly sustained Army training project in the peacetime history of the United States has had a proven impact on the Army's ability to fight and win. It also demonstrates that innovation in a process, such as training, can have an affect every bit as significant as advances in weapons, tactics, or organizational structure.

---

[6] Chapman, *Origins and Development*, pp.14–23; TRADOC Annual Command History, CY 1991, p.156, Office of the Command Historian, TRADOC, Fort Monroe, Va.

CONCLUSION

Jon T. Hoffman

Both business and military thinkers have developed theories of innovation that attempt to explain past success and serve as a model for future effort. This survey of U.S. Army innovation, however, highlights the difficulty of determining lessons that can be applied in a concrete fashion to guide behavior. As the examples illustrate, the development of a new capability comes in many forms and via many paths, with one experience often contradicting another.

The twin histories of the tank destroyer and tank warfare, for example, offer evidence pointing in opposite directions. Historians seem to agree that the establishment of the independent Armored Force in July 1940 was a key element in breaking the conservative stranglehold of the infantry and cavalry branches that had stifled progress. Giving the Armored Force the power to develop doctrine and organization and control its own training allowed American capability in the field to catch up with and, in some areas, eventually surpass foreign rivals. Less than two years later, the Army followed a similar model in establishing the Tank Destroyer Center, yet this effort produced failure.

Perhaps the difference in the two cases is simple. Whereas the Armored Force built upon the demonstrated success of blitzkrieg, making improvements at the margin in such areas as task organization and greater mechanization, the Tank Destroyer Center struck out on an entirely novel and untried path, taking a gamble that carried greater risk of error. The antitank concept ultimately failed because it proved to be a bad idea.

A similar contrast in process arises from the experiences of the Armored Force and the air observation post. In the case of the tank, the infantry and cavalry branches both proved incapable of adapting to a new weapon that fell outside their traditional areas of expertise. The field artillery, on the other hand, not only saw the value of aircraft in improving the timeliness and accuracy of fire support but also aggressively pursued this new capability in the face of strident opposition from the aviation community.

These examples further reveal no particular pattern to the source of innovation, even with regard to scale. Armored warfare had no single father, but benefited from a number of champions, most of whom had long-standing connections with mechanized forces and were senior in rank. Interestingly enough, the primary bureaucratic facilitator was General Andrews, an aviator with little or no experience in this field. Nevertheless, it was practitioners in the operating forces, not planners in the service headquarters, who pushed the new concept. Airmobility, on the other hand, sprang largely from officers who were closely associated with the Army Staff's Aviation Directorate. General Howze, the prime proponent, was a cavalry and armor officer new to the aviation field, while Colonel Williams had begun his career as an artilleryman. The tank destroyer concept seemed to arise from the highest echelons of all, with Generals Marshall and McNair pushing a new idea that had no real constituency anywhere in the Army. The only common ground in these examples of big innovation is the obvious factor that they required support from senior leaders to become reality. But the ideas and the initiative also came from the same higher echelons rather than from younger officers who, as many theorists believe, are more attuned to emerging methods of warfare.

The source of smaller innovations spans the entire spectrum—from individuals to large groups, from the front lines to research agencies in the rear. Each innovation seems to have developed in an almost unique way. The air observation post makes one of the most intriguing cases. Although the idea had high-level support, lower-ranking officers played major roles in developing the concept and making it a reality.

While the Ordnance Department came up with the first widely fielded semiautomatic rifle (as one would expect it should), the entire effort centered on one man who not only invented the weapon itself but also the machine tools needed to reliably manufacture it. The Ordnance Department likewise was searching for a lightweight antitank weapon when it got the bazooka, but the latter resulted from individual initiative and was in competition with the official focus on a spigot mortar. Nevertheless, the establishment played a major role, developing the shaped-charge projectile and informing the rocket group about the new round. That accomplishment made the bazooka possible, because a launcher and rocket without the right warhead would have been useless.

In retrospect, the bazooka seemed like a long overdue weapon. Its component technologies had been well known for some time, and armies had been evaluating means to fight tanks for a generation. But for most of the two decades after World War I, the standard weapons of the day were sufficient to penetrate the thin armor then in use. And no one had yet proven in battle that the tank would dominate. Thus one would have needed considerable foresight to begin looking for a solution to a novel problem that would only crop up in the future. Even the German army, the interwar leader in armored warfare, would end up using an anti-aircraft gun as its primary antitank weapon during World War II because it had not thought to develop a better defensive system to deal with the offensive capability it was creating.

The marriage of two or more existing weapons or pieces of equipment to produce a new or enhanced capability is another frequent thread. The Ordnance Department almost certainly would have fielded an upgunned amphibian at some point once battle experience demonstrated the limitations of the 37-mm. version. Colonel Triplet's achievement lay in seeing the need for such a capability even before the lighter-armed vehicle was in combat and then coming up with a solution that could be procured immediately. To its credit, the Army moved rapidly to turn that idea into reality. Likewise the airborne radio direction finding setup consisted entirely of existing electronic components married to an airframe. The result was a radical new capability that cost very little time and money to develop. The field artillery actually took a step backwards in terms of technical capability when it adopted light civilian aircraft, but coupling them with the latest radios proved effective. The National Training Center adapted a fairly small system for training a handful of pilots into a much more elaborate scheme that could prepare thousands of soldiers at a time for the reality of war. It also joined together different solutions to disparate problems (inadequate training methods and training areas, lack of training realism) to create a system that both solved the individual issues and produced benefits greater than the sum of its parts.

While the focus of innovation is often on technology, advances also arise from a mix of new equipment, new doctrine or procedures, and new organizational structure. The increase in field artillery capability came not just from the acquisition of light planes and modern radios but equally as much from their incorporation within the artillery battalions and the adoption of improved fire direction techniques. The significance of the organizational aspect is highlighted by the British experience, which did not produce similarly impressive results. The U.S. Army succeeded in World War II with a mediocre tank in part because it ultimately developed better unit structure and doctrine than its allies and enemies. The airmobile concept may have been built around the helicopter, but the innovative aspects were all organizational and doctrinal. The Benning revolution and the National Training Center demonstrate that even the methods used to prepare soldiers and their leaders for war are subject to innovation and can have a major impact on battlefield success.

Sometimes the choice of how to proceed in developing or implementing a new capability played a significant role. For the bazooka, Colonel Skinner's initiative in joining the spigot mortar shoot-off made a big difference. He short-circuited the bureaucracy and proved the weapon's effectiveness in front of senior leaders, resulting in an immediate procurement decision. With airborne radio direction finding, engineers from two agencies teamed up to find the solution, eventually focusing on the method initially deemed least likely to succeed from a technical standpoint. Most important, having built a practical system, the engineers deployed with it to the field and oversaw its installation and initial employment. That enabled them to correct the problems that arose in combat.

The airborne radio direction finder demonstrated another important factor—the effect of response to failure during the ultimate test of war. The diligence of the engineers in seeking out the cause of problems during initial field trials in Vietnam prevented the system from being written off. Likewise the poor performance of air observation posts in North Africa might have doomed the concept, but officers and men in the midst of combat adapted their theories and methods to fit reality and made the system work. While the tank destroyer program never approached the capability its proponents expected, it still produced a worthwhile contribution to the combined arms team in the form of an effective assault gun (something the German army specifically developed as a valued asset).

While some innovations ultimately fail the test of war, many others face an even more grueling road simply getting beyond the inspiration stage. Early innovation theorist Alfred North

Whitehead observed that turning an idea into a practical capability is often "a process of disciplined attack upon one difficulty after another."[1] Garand spent twenty years perfecting his rifle before it was ready for field use. Lest anyone think that was a simple or inevitable process, many others—civilian and military—around the world were attempting to achieve the same objective but did not get there before him. The scientific principles behind radar were relatively easy to work out once physicists and engineers began focusing on the concept, but it took years of painstaking trial and error to develop a useful device. In Vietnam, the men of Battery B, 8th Battalion, 6th Artillery, made numerous changes until they had a speed shifter that met all their requirements, benefiting from the ability to test each new iteration in actual operations and identify shortcomings.

A final recurring theme is the element of chance in determining the outcome of the development process. Luck struck the radar program several times. The basic idea for the capability came from an unexpected result of a Navy experiment for an unrelated purpose. A ground soldier, trying to outdo his aviation counterparts, made radar look more effective than it actually was in front of senior leadership, and that helped bring more money to the program and speed up development. No one thought of radar as an aid to navigation until a target aircraft went astray, but that event gave rise to an entirely new use for the system. Recognizing the role of luck, of course, is not particularly helpful because one cannot institutionalize it or plan for it in the innovation process. But it is important to realize that factors that cannot be controlled are often decisive.

As the examples in this volume bear out, innovation arises from a wide range of sources and processes. Each brings certain strengths and weaknesses, though these characteristics are not universal and determinative even in apparently similar situations. If anything, history indicates that there is no single or reliable path to success. For every prospective rule, there is usually an exception. It is thus difficult, if not impossible, to develop a useful grand theory of innovation or a list of prescriptions for fostering positive change. The only constant seems to be that a resourceful and adaptive military is likely to fare better than competitors who take

---

[1] As quoted in David C. Mowery and Nathan Rosenberg, *Paths of Innovation: Technological Change in 20th-Century America* (New York: Cambridge University Press, 1998), p. 1.

a more conservative approach—though the tank destroyer force is a reminder that not all innovation will prove successful.

Henry Ford, famous for turning the assembly line into a staple of manufacturing, perhaps captured the one irrefutable principle of innovation: "It could almost be written down as a formula that when a man begins to think that he has at last found his method, he had better begin a most searching examination of himself to see whether some part of his brain has not gone to sleep."[2]

---

[2] As quoted in Richard N. Foster, *Innovation: The Attacker's Advantage* (New York: Summit Books, 1986), p. 22.

SUGGESTED READINGS

M1 Garand Rifle

Green, Constance McLaughlin, Harry C. Thomson, and Peter C. Roots. *The Ordnance Department: Planning Munitions for War.* United States Army in World War II. Washington D.C.: Office of the Chief of Military History, Department of the Army, 1955.

Hatcher, Julian S. *The Book of The Garand.* Washington, D.C.: Infantry Journal Press, 1948.

McCarten, John. "The Man Behind the Gun," *New Yorker*, 6 February 1943, pp. 22–28.

Radar

Brown, Louis. *A Radar History of World War II: Technical and Military Imperatives.* London: Taylor and Francis, 1999.

Zahl, Harold A. *Electrons Away or Tales of a Government Scientist.* New York: Vantage Press, 1968.

The Benning Revolution

Bland, Larry I. "George C. Marshall and the Education of Army Leaders." *Military Review* 68 (October 1988): 27–37.

Pogue, Forrest C., *George C. Marshall: Education of a General, 1880–1939.* New York: Viking Press, 1963.

Air Observation Posts

Dastrup, Boyd L. *King of Battle: A Branch History of the U.S. Army's Field Artillery.* Washington, D.C.: U.S. Army Center of Military History, 1993.

Raines Jr., Edgar F. *Eyes of Artillery: The Origins of Modern U.S. Army Aviation in World War II.* Army Historical Series. Washington, D.C.: U.S. Army Center of Military History, 2000.

Wakefield, Ken. *The Fighting Grasshoppers: U.S. Liaison Aircraft Operations in Europe, 1942–1945.* Stillwater, Minn.: Specialty Press, 1990.

Armored Force Organization

Gillie, Mildred H. *Forging the Thunderbolt: History of the U.S. Army's Armored Forces, 1917–1945.* Mechanicsburg, Pa.: Stackpole Books, 2006.

Hofmann, George F. *Through Mobility We Conquer: The Mechanization of U.S. Cavalry.* Lexington: University Press of Kentucky, 2006.

Hofmann, George F., and Donn A. Starry, eds. *Camp Colt to Desert Storm: The History of U.S. Armored Forces.* Lexington: University Press of Kentucky, 1999.

Johnson, David E. *Fast Tanks and Heavy Bombers: Innovation in the U.S. Army, 1917–1945.* Ithaca, N.Y.: Cornell University Press, 2003.

Tank Destroyer Force

Baily, Charles M. *Faint Praise: American Tanks and Tank Destroyers During World War II.* Hamden, Conn.: Archon, 1983.

Gabel, Christopher R. *Seek, Strike, and Destroy: U.S. Army Tank Destroyer Doctrine in World War II.* Fort Leavenworth, Kans.: U.S. Army Command and General Staff College, 1985.

The Bazooka

Green, Constance McLaughlin, Harry C. Thomson, and Peter C. Roots, *The Ordnance Department: Planning Munitions For War.* United States Army in World War II. Washington, D.C.: Office of the Chief of Military History, Department of the Army, 1955.

Rottman, Gordon L. *World War II Infantry Anti-Tank Tactics (Elite).* Oxford, U.K.: Osprey Publishing, 2005.

Upgunning the Amphibian Tank

Croizat, Victor J. *Across the Reef: The Amphibious Tracked Vehicle at War.* Quantico, Va.: Marine Corps Association, 1992.

Triplet, William S. *A Colonel in the Armored Divisions: A Memoir, 1941–1945.* Columbia: University of Missouri Press, 2001.

Conquering the Hedgerows

Blumenson, Martin. *Breakout and Pursuit*. United States Army in World War II. Washington, D.C.: Office of the Chief of Military History, 1961.

Carafano, James J. *GI Ingenuity: Improvisation, Technology, and Winning World War II*. Westport, Conn.: Praeger, 2006.

Doubler, Michael D. *Closing with the Enemy: How GIs Fought the War in Europe, 1944–1945*. Lawrence: University Press of Kansas, 1994.

Special Patrol Groups

Donnelly, William M. "'The Best Army That Can Be Put in the Field in the Circumstances:' The U.S. Army, July 1951–July 1953." *Journal of Military History* 71 (July 2007): 809–47.

Hackworth, David H., and Julie Sherman, *About Face: The Odyssey of an American Warrior*. New York: Simon and Schuster, 1989.

Hogan, David W. *Raiders or Elite Infantry? The Changing Role of the U.S. Army Rangers from Dieppe to Grenada* (Westport, Conn.: Greenwood Press, 1992)

Airmobility

Cheng, Christopher C. S. *Air Mobility: The Development of a Doctrine*. Westport, Conn.: Praeger, 1994.

Galvin, John R. *Air Assault: The Development of Airmobile Warfare*. New York: Hawthorne Books, 1969.

Howze, Hamilton H. *A Cavalryman's Story: Memoirs of a Twentieth-Century Army General*. Washington, D.C.: Smithsonian Institution Press, 1996.

Moore, Harold G., and Joseph L. Galloway, *We Were Soldiers Once . . . and Young: Ia Drang—The Battle That Changed the War in Vietnam*. New York: Random House, 1992.

Airborne Radio Direction Finding

Gilbert, James L. *The Most Secret War: Army Signals Intelligence in Vietnam*. Fort Belvoir, Va.: U.S. Army Intelligence and Security Command, 2003.

Hanyok, Robert J. *Spartans in Darkness: American SIGNIT and the Indochina War, 1945–1975*. [Fort Meade, Md.:] Center for Cryptologic History, National Security Agency, 2002.

Artillery Speed Shifter

Foster, Nathaniel W. "Speed Shifting the 155-mm. Howitzer, Towed: The Evolution of an Idea." *Artillery Trends*, January 1967, p. 17.

Hay Jr., John H. *Tactical and Materiel Innovations*. Vietnam Studies. Washington, D.C.: Department of the Army, 1974.

Ott, David E. *Field Artillery, 1954–1973*. Washington, D.C.: Department of the Army, 1975.

National Training Center

Chapman, Anne W. *The National Training Center Matures, 1985–1993*. Fort Monroe, Va.: U.S. Army Training and Doctrine Command, 1997.

————. *The Origins and Development of the National Training Center*. Fort Monroe, Va.: U.S. Army Training and Doctrine Command, 1992.

Conclusion

Murray, Williamson, and Allan R. Millett, eds. *Military Innovation in the Interwar Period*. New York: Cambridge University Press, 1996.

Posen, Barry R. *The Sources of Military Doctrine: France, Britain, and Germany Between the World Wars*. Ithaca, N.Y.: Cornell University Press, 1984.

Rosen, Stephen P. *Winning the Next War: Innovation and the Modern Military*. Ithaca, N.Y.: Cornell University Press, 1991.

Winton, Harold R., and David R. Mets. *The Challenge of Change: Military Institutions and New Realities, 1918–1941*. Lincoln: University of Nebraska Press, 2000.

INDEX